A GRIEF UN-VEILED

~FIFTEEN YEARS LATER~

A GRIEF UN-VEILED

ONE FATHER'S JOURNEY
THROUGH THE DEATH OF A CHILD

~FIFTEEN YEARS LATER~

Gregory Floyd

Foreword by Thomas Howard

PARACLETE PRESS
Brewster, Massachusetts

2012   First Printing This Edition

Copyright © 2012, 1999 by Gregory Floyd

ISBN: 978-1-61261-239-3

The Library of Congress has catalogued the original edition of this book as follows:

Library of Congress Cataloging-in-Publication Data

Floyd, Gregory, 1954–
    A grief unveiled : one father's journey through the death of a child / Gregory Floyd.
        p.   cm.
    ISBN 1-55725-215-7 (pbk.)
        1. Floyd, Gregory, 1954–   . 2. Fathers and sons. 3. Bereavement—Religious aspects—Catholic Church. 4. Grief—Religious aspects—Catholic Church. 5. Consolation. I. Title.
    BX4705.F6134A3   1999
    248.8'66'092—dc21   99-11221
    [B]   CIP

10 9 8 7 6 5 4 3 2 1

Published by Paraclete Press
Brewster, Massachusetts
www.paracletepress.com

Printed in the United States of America

To Maureen,

strength like a rock
laughter like a mountain stream
love like a garden somewhere in Eden

and to our children

Gregory
Thérèse
David
Rose
Susanna
Nicole
Catherine
and
Maria

without whom the world would be such a grayer,
dimmer place.

CONTENTS

FOREWORD

I have never met Gregory and Maureen Floyd. And yet I consider them to be among my most cherished friends. We have spoken on the phone many times, and exchanged letters. I have listened (with unabashedly flowing tears) to Gregory's tape of songs which he wrote not long ago.

About what? And whence this odd friendship? Ah: there is the key.

It is all about the sudden death of their little boy John-Paul, struck by a car in front of their house in a quiet cul-de-sac, and killed instantly. His brother David was with him and was also hit, but survived.

All of us, I think, and especially us parents, would place the death of one of our children at the top of the list of unimaginable horrors. War, famine, betrayal, estrangement, death—these are all there on that list. But there is something about the poignance, the grotesque irony, and the clashing contradiction that swirl about the death of a small child, especially an angelic child, which John-Paul happens to have been—there is something about this that complicates and intensifies and batters at our grief in a unique way.

Gregory Floyd, in the book you are about to read, has charted, with remorseless candor, immense courage, and acute notation of every nuance, the progress (if that is the word) of the grief that overwhelmed him in the days, weeks, months, and now years, that followed John-Paul's death. I say overwhelmed *him:* Maureen is very, very much at the center of the picture. But Gregory confesses over and over that he, the father and man, cannot quite enter wholly into the fathomless mystery that marks the grief of a mother. This couple knows, if anyone ever has, what it means to be one heart and one flesh in the holy sacrament of marriage. And yet death, that great Enemy, has among his cruel tactics, the power to drive a wedge even here, so that there is a dread sense in which each must bear his own grief, even in the midst of bearing one another's burden.

The following record is a very rich one. Gregory Floyd is a man who knows God, like Job or John the Baptist. Hence, there is nothing saccharine or tawdry here (it is so easy to gild death with sentimentalism), nor any pyrotechnics. It is a straightforward and unsparing record—unsparing of the reader as well as of the writer, I might add. Nothing is swept under the rug. No platitudes are brought into play to ameliorate things. The boy is dead. An outrage has torn at the fabric of the universe. An obscenity (yes—an obscenity) has stained Creation. Mere palliatives and placebos won't do. We go down into the valley of the shadow of death with this family—nay, we might even say to Hell, following the Pioneer of our Faith as he descends on Holy Saturday to the extremity of the mystery.

There is an interesting note that strides like a motif all the way through this account. It is this: No matter how high-flown or deep-probing Gregory's reflections and cries of agony are, and no matter what spiritual immensities are invoked, we are never, for a single page, removed from the the immediate, tangible, physical reality of John-Paul's death. There is no threshold between the spiritual and the physical here. The one bespeaks the other. This is because Gregory is a sacramentalist, and hence is utterly at home in those precincts where the eye of faith sees the eternal in the temporal. We never leave that little boy, eventually buried in his coffin, for two minutes. There is an incomprehensible disjuncture, of course, between the simultaneous facts of John-Paul's body in the cold earth and his being safely home with Jesus and His Blessed Mother— even in the "lap" of the Father, we are told more than once. But this is not a contradiction. The disjuncture stretches our faith and toughens it, getting us ready for that great Consummation of all things when we will see how everything fits.

The reader will find himself pricked by the needle-sharp perspicacity of Gregory's insights, and also of his probing and doubts. He (the reader, that is) will find himself drawn into somber reflections about the mysteries of God—of God as loving Father (then why did he let this happen?), and as Sovereign (then why did he let this happen?). He will find himself challenged by reflections on Scripture that penetrate far beyond the cavalier reading we are likely to give Scripture when all is going brightly for us. And dreams—lots of dreams. What about dreams in the life of a Christian? It becomes clear that more than a few of them come from a Source infinitely higher than anything poor Sigmund Freud ever fancied.

And what about "healing"? How fast should it occur? Are there temptations to dawdle, or to hold on to one's grief as a sort of cockade in one's hat, giving one special status? How does one orchestrate one's own broken heart while still having to be fully father to a houseful of surviving children, and husband to a grieving mother?

The prose in this book is often positively gnomic (a nice, ancient word suggesting compact, incisive, "repeatable" lines). For example: "There is a difference between early grief and later grief. Early grief is acute; later grief is more diffuse. Early grief smacks, stings, punches; later grief is more gentle. Early grief is a stalker; later grief is a companion. Early grief is crags and crevices; later grief is furrows softened by the passage of time."

One more thing: the songs. Here we find lyrics wrung from the depths of a bereaved father's heart-songs of sorrow, of love, of wistfulness, but then of hope and even—yes—joy. I have had the privilege of hearing these evocative lyrics sung when I set aside one Sunday afternoon to listen to Gregory's album, *Angel in Disguise*. When it was finished, I rang Gregory to tell him how much it had meant to me. But he had to interpret my sobs, for I could not speak.

Read this book, and be drawn along the Way of the Cross.

Thomas Howard
Manchester, MA

ACKNOWLEDGMENTS

I would like to express my gratitude and appreciation
to Mrs. Eleanor Benson,
who first took my handwritten notes on yellow legal pads
and brought order out of chaos;
to Mrs. Binnie Burke,
who taught John-Paul and who typed
and retyped the entire manuscript as a labor of love;
to Lillian Miao,
publisher of Paraclete Press
who believed there was a story to tell here;
to Professor Tom Howard,
who wrote the foreword and
whose friendship has been a singular source of grace;
to Father Robert Oliver, JCL, STD,
of the Brotherhood of Hope, for his theological expertise and
profound love, support, and encouragement; and finally,
to Patricia Klein,
whose honesty, integrity, compassion, humor,
and consummate editorial skill helped bring this book to fruition.

John-Paul Floyd
October 19, 1988–April 25, 1995

A GRIEF UN-
VEILED

Your Cross

The everlasting God has in His wisdom foreseen from eternity the cross
that he now presents to you as a gift from His inmost heart.
This cross he now sends you he has considered with his all-knowing eyes,
understood with His divine mind, tested with His wise justice,
warmed with loving arms and weighed with His own hands to see that
it be not one inch too large and not one ounce too heavy for you.
He has blessed it with His holy name, anointed it with His grace,
perfumed it with His consolation, taken one last glance at you and your courage,
and then sent it to you from heaven,
a special greeting from God to you,
an alms of the all-merciful love of God.

—St. Francis de Sales

Blessed is the man
Who walks in your favor
Who loves all your words
And hides them
like treasure.
In the darkest place
Of his desperate heart,
They are a light
A strong, sure light.

*—Fernando Ortega and John Andrew Schreiner,
from* Lord of Eternity

ONE

Changed Forever in an Instant

The weekend had been marvelous. A retreat for Christian men focused on some of the critical issues of masculinity in contemporary society: being a son, fatherhood, sexuality, male passivity, forgiveness, prayer, and union with God. It was a weekend of healing and grace, as we looked to Jesus Christ as the model of masculinity as well as its Creator, Savior, and Lord. We prayed and talked together as Christian men about the things we desperately need to talk about but rarely do.

The weekend had been bracing, deep, with a tremendous spirit of openness. God had been on the move, to restore and reconcile. It was a privilege to be part of the team, to watch the truth of the gospel and the power of the Holy Spirit to change men's hearts. It also had meant, however, that I had spent another weekend away from my wife, Maureen, and our children, and I decided to take the following Monday off from work.

It was April 24, 1995, and the children were on Easter break from school. There were seven of them, ranging in age from ten down to six weeks: Gregory, Thérèse, David, John-Paul, Rose, Susanna, and Nicole, our newborn. They are high-spirited, usually happy, and sometimes overwhelming in sheer energy and numbers. That very morning Maureen was feeling exhausted. At 10:30 in the morning I walked into the kitchen, and she said to

1

me, "I can't take this anymore. Everyone's screaming, everyone's at me. Everyone has needs at the same time. . . ."

"Come on," I said, "let's put the kids in the car, buy some sandwiches, and go for a picnic." Even though she did not want to, Maureen acquiesced. We piled in the car, picked up the sandwiches, and took off for the park.

The day was bright and breezy. We sat around the picnic table talking, laughing, and eating. Everyone took turns catching Susanna, who was almost two and who kept running away from the table. After lunch we played freeze tag on the jungle gym. Maureen was relaxed again and the strain had left her face. These are the shining points in time that make the strains and sacrifices of having a large family worth the effort, because the joy is multiplied by every laughing, smiling face, by the grace of every supple limb in motion. It was one of those rare, perfect moments.

As nap time drew near, we headed home. Maureen put Rose and Susanna down and asked me to take the baby, Nicole. We went to the family room and I laid down on the couch with her. Gregory was out with friends. Thérèse was drawing. John-Paul and David were in the basement playing with their "guys": all the little GI Joes, space cadets, Power Rangers, and other creatures that boys play with.

Nicole was awake, so I took her into the kitchen. Our house has a strange feature: The kitchen is in the front, looking out onto the street. It is a quiet, dead-end street with only 13 houses. Lots of children live on it, and the neighbors know to drive slowly and be on the lookout when they reach the middle of the block. At 3:20 the doorbell rang. I was annoyed because whoever it was kept pressing the bell, and I had warned the children not to ring the bell during nap time. I thought I was going downstairs to correct someone. I was wrong.

In a voice hysterical with fear, a handsome young man yelled, "Oh my God, come quickly, I think I just hit your kids!" I ran upstairs to give the baby to Thérèse who had heard something and was starting to get upset. "No!" I said sternly. "That is not going to help. You take Nicole and sit right there." I flew down the stairs and ran outside. There in the middle of the street was a stopped car. Further down the road on our front lawn, lay our two boys, David and John-Paul. The young man was beside himself.

I ran inside and called 911 and told them our address, "two boys hit," and so forth. Then I ran upstairs and yelled to Maureen, "Honey, get up. The boys have been hit!" I flew back outside. David was crying and moaning. His head was bloody but he was making sounds. By this time Maureen was running out the door.

"Go to David," I said. I ran back to John-Paul. His lips were turning blue. "Johnny, please," I begged, "come on, little boy." I had my hand on his chest underneath his shirt. I could feel his heart beating, but he was not breathing. By this time several neighbors had appeared. One knelt down next to me. "Is he breathing?" he asked. "I can't feel anything." I had my face next to his, straining to feel his breath against mine. No breath. "Should I give him mouth-to-mouth?" I asked. "Yes, try it."

So there, kneeling on the front lawn, I gave John-Paul mouth-to-mouth resuscitation. His chest would fill up with my breath, expand and contract, expand and contract. "Come on, Johnny. . . . That's a good boy, Johnny. . . . Please, Johnny. . . . You can do it, little boy." I could say nothing else, over and over again.

The rescue squad arrived in two trucks, with two teams. One started working on David, the other on John-Paul. I looked over at Maureen. Never have I seen such a look of horror and love combined as I saw on her face.

3

There was a lot of commotion as the rescue squad, the police, and the medical intensive care unit did their respective jobs and tried to figure out where to take the boys. I was so intensely focused on them that many things I heard did not register completely, except for two: What needs to be done here? What's the best thing for the boys?

Confusion reigned. We heard "helicopter." We heard "Robert Wood Johnson Hospital." We heard "Overlook Hospital." We heard "Pennsylvania." We heard "Newark Trauma Center." Then we heard the boys were going to two different hospitals. "Wait a minute," I said. "Let's just make sure the boys go to the same hospital. We don't need to add a commute on top of everything else." But that was not to be.

All the while they were working on John-Paul. I had stopped giving him mouth-to-mouth resuscitation and they were giving him oxygen. They brought a stretcher, and we carefully lifted him onto it and placed him in the ambulance. I told Maureen that we were going to Overlook Hospital and that she and David were going to University Hospital in Newark, a distance of about fifteen miles. Somewhere in the midst of all this I asked our neighbor Janet to take the rest of the children. Janet had been talking with Johnny only a half hour earlier.

As I took off, my last picture was of Maureen cradling David's wounded body, grief and shock etched into her features. We still were not sure where we were going. The medical intensive care unit folks were saying "New Brunswick." I said, "Overlook on Route 78 is faster." So with police escort we headed for Overlook. I was tying the stretcher to the bed with strips of cloth so it would not move. I rode in the ambulance at the feet of my son, saying, "Come on, little boy, come on, Johnny, you can do it," and in my heart saying, "Oh God, please. . . ."

We pulled up to the emergency room and took the stretcher through the doors. A team of doctors and nurses was waiting for us. There was a chief of operations, who was giving orders and directing traffic, as well as other doctors and nurses. They cut off Johnny's clothes, and I watched as they made an incision in his groin and stuck a long tube into him. A nurse was telling me what was going on. I could not take my eyes off him. One doctor held a mask over his face and kept pumping oxygen. After the initial investigation, they took him for a CAT scan. As I waited outside the room, family and friends began to arrive.

The long watch had begun. At some point later in the afternoon, after the initial diagnosis, a doctor came into the room where we were sitting. I said to him, "Doctor, these are my friends. It would be most helpful if you'd tell us exactly how things are with John-Paul."

He said, "The situation is very serious. You have a very sick little boy. Only time will tell. The next twenty-four hours are critical." "Is he not breathing on his own?" I asked. "No, he's not," he replied. "Is he in a coma?" "Yes."

Coma. The word is dark, sinister, and foreboding. It hit me in the gut. It was at once monstrous and amorphous, like an arching shadow sucking the light out of my mind. My son is not conscious, I think to myself. My son cannot breathe. My son is lying on a stretcher with a machine moving his chest up and down. He cannot think or feel or speak and the device that measures his brain activity registers no movement.

I called the emergency room in Newark to find Maureen and check on David. When she came to the phone I asked, "Are your parents there?" "Yes." "Go get them." I wanted them standing near her. "How's David?" I asked when she returned. "It looks like he is going to be okay. Bruises and lacerations, but nothing is broken."

"How's Johnny?" "Honey, Johnny's in a coma. He's not breathing on his own. He's a very sick little boy and the doctor said the next twenty-four hours are critical. I think you'd better come up here."

I was with Johnny all night long, back and forth from our room to his. Someone had brought the baby to Maureen and we kept her with us. A few times during the night I tried to lie down and rest. Rest was futile. Maureen and I looked at each other. "What's going to happen to our little boy?" she asked.

I could not rest. I could hardly talk and sometimes I wondered that I could breathe. I found myself looking for other, deeper breaths because of the pressure I felt on my chest. Then the ground would shift and I would begin to feel some of the weight of what was happening. But it was not possible to take it all in.

At that moment I was straddling two realities. I was in shock, and my bodily mechanisms were shielding my mind from taking in more of the unbearable than it could handle. I was hoping that this would not be what it looked like. At the same time I was intensely present to what was going on—so present that all I could see was the beautiful face of my son, his freckles, his hair, his lips, the feel of his skin as I kissed him and whispered in his ear, "Come on, Johnny, you can do it, come on, little boy, wake up." I was aware of the whir of machinery, the different colored lights, the doctors and nurses. But there was a shield around us. It was made of everything that is fatherly. It was made of love and afforded us complete privacy so I could keep talking to him as though the strength of my love could wake him from the ominous sleep that had engulfed him.

I focused on him, touching him, kissing him, talking gently in his ear—anything to try to communicate that I was there and that I loved him and that he was surrounded by love.

His chest moved rhythmically up and down and his color was normal though his bruises were starting to appear and his broken leg was being wired by a doctor. But the eyes: I pressed open his eyelids. Light did not affect them and touch did not affect them. I looked into them and they registered nothing. They were there but they were not there. They were vacant, and in the pit of my soul I knew he was not going to make it. This boy of mine was not going to wake up. This child was going to die.

As morning came and light filtered into the room, my father-in-law and I drove to Newark to get David. His grandmother had stayed with him overnight. He was extremely timid and was walking like a ninety-year-old man. The nurse said he was fine. In fact, she had to move his limbs to show him that nothing was broken. She said he was afraid that he might hurt himself and that his body was full of tension from the accident. I walked with him and helped him into the car. We drove home to get the other children. The first question everyone had was, "How's Johnny? Is he all right?" I said to them one by one, "Let's get everybody together and then I'll tell you all at once."

Finally we were all together: Gregory, Thérèse, David, Rose, and Susanna. Maureen and the baby were at the hospital. I took a deep breath and said a quick prayer before telling the children, "Johnny is very sick." I let that sink in for a few moments. "I'm going to take you all to the hospital with me so you can see him and touch him and talk to him."

We got in two cars and drove off. When we arrived, the children were hungry, so I bought them some milkshakes. Then we went upstairs to the Pediatric Intensive Care Unit. The hallway was lined with family and friends quietly praying, quietly waiting, hoping against hope. The children greeted their mother and the baby, and then we sat together in the room where Maureen and I had spent the night.

"Children, I need to tell you a few things. Johnny is very sick and he's probably going to die." They started crying. "It's okay to cry. You can cry as much as you like because it's a very sad time. It's a very sad time for Mommy and Daddy, too. I want to tell you what Johnny's going to look like. First, he's lying on a bed. He's covered with a sheet, just like at home. He looks like he's asleep, and he has a lot of wires attached to him. The wires don't hurt him. They help the doctors and the nurses to know how he's doing and whether he needs anything. And Johnny's not in any pain, so you don't have to worry about that."

Someone took the baby and we walked down the hallway—Maureen, I, and the children. When we were in the room, I said, "Now get around the bed where you can see him and touch him." We all got as near to John-Paul as we could. Our four-year-old, Rose, was sitting on the bed near his feet, and the others were standing around their brother. The whole family was crying except for Rose, who did not fully understand everything that was happening. The nurses were crying. The priest was crying. I said, "Let's each take a turn and talk to Johnny and tell him anything we'd like." "Johnny, you're such a good brother." "Johnny, please don't die." "I love you so much, Johnny." Over and over they kept saying the same things, weeping and tenderly touching his arms, his legs, his face. Maureen and I knew we needed to let this moment linger as long as needed, suspended between heaven and earth. At a certain point I said, "Children, let's pray now. This is our last family prayer time with Johnny. Let's sing whatever he'd like to sing." So we sang "Shine, Jesus, Shine" and a few of his other favorites. Toward the end, Gregory said, "I think we should tell

John-Paul we're sorry and ask his forgiveness for anything we ever said or did to him that wasn't loving." We each asked his forgiveness. It was a moment of profound grace, coming from his ten-year-old brother. Then I said to them, "Why don't you say anything else you'd like to say to Johnny and give him a kiss good-bye." Each of the children walked over to his head and bent down and spoke quietly in his ear and kissed him good-bye. We left the Pediatric Intensive Care Unit and walked back to our room. Somebody took the children home, and Maureen and I maintained the remainder of our bedside vigil.

At about 3:00 P.M. a doctor and a nurse came to talk to us. The doctor began with some preliminary remarks about the fact that there was no easy way to say what he was about to say. He told us that John-Paul was brain dead and then explained what that meant, so as to assure us that he was really and truly dead. He then moved the conversation in the direction of the nurse, Cecilia, who was the organ transplant coordinator. Cecilia explained organ donation and asked us if we would like to donate any of John-Paul's organs or tissue. We said yes, and she then explained the procedure of "harvesting" the organs. She also mentioned the possibility of coming back to hold him once the harvesting had taken place. She said the surgery would start around 10:00 P.M. and be completed by 3:00 A.M. When she had finished, the doctor said, "I know no good can come of this for John-Paul, but at least some good can come of this for someone else." "Doctor," I said quietly, "I have to disagree with you. We're a Christian family and we believe that great good can come of this. We believe that our son is in heaven and that we're going to see him again." Then I said, "Can we go say good-bye?" Gesturing toward our family and friends, I said, "This is our family, and we'd like them to come, too." We walked back up the hallway into Johnny's room. There must have been twenty of us. We prayed quietly for a few minutes. Maureen and I stood there at his bed, barely taking in the enormity of what had just happened to us in one twenty-four-hour period. I invited everyone to say something to Johnny, to pray to him, and to kiss him good-bye. Then we left. We went home to see the children and to prepare for our final chance to hold him, which would be at 3:00 A.M.

As it turned out, John-Paul had been dead on our front lawn, his brain stem snapped by the impact of the car. And in that instant, our lives had changed forever.

TWO

Ascending Calvary

As we arrived home, people started coming to the door. "Maryann and I are bringing dinner tonight." "Nancy's bringing dinner tomorrow." "Give me your laundry." "I'll take your ironing." My parents came over to do whatever we needed and to spend the night so we could go back to the hospital.

In the midst of shock, suddenly a host of details needed immediate attention. A funeral on Friday meant a wake Wednesday night and Thursday. It was then Tuesday afternoon. Somebody called the funeral home and arranged for me to pick out a casket. Dad said, "I'll go with you." Here we were, twenty-eight hours after the accident, driving to the funeral home to arrange for a funeral and pick out a casket.

Pick out a casket. For my son. I could not even take in the words as I said them. I said to my father, "I can't believe we're doing this." We met with a young woman who helped us with the details. Coffins, from $600 to $10,000 . . . wood . . . metal . . . with satin . . . with brass. They even come airtight, so the elements will not affect their contents. I said to her, "I want the simplest, plainest, most modest one you have. He's not going to be in there forever." Fortunately, they had an unadorned white box for a child. In the only moment of comic relief we had I asked her, "Why would someone spend $10,000 on a box that's going in the ground?" "They're nuts," she replied.

As we arrived home my brothers began to show up. Every time I looked at Mark he was on the verge of tears. Justin was calling friends in England, Ireland, and throughout the United States and Canada. Brendan was on his way from San Francisco. Rick would be over soon. Friends started calling from all over as the news spread. Mom was running interference on the telephone. Annie, our dear friend from Mexico, came over to take care of the children for the week. Somewhere in the back of my mind I realized I was experiencing the Body of Christ at work.

We had to go to bed. Maureen was nursing Nicole and needed to rest to have enough milk for the baby. We both wanted to close our eyes and wish away this horror. I said to Maureen, "I feel like I'm an actor in someone else's drama." That was what it felt like. I could not believe that this was happening to us. We were going through motions that had no relationship to our normal life. Maureen said, "I keep hoping I'm going to wake up from this and find it was a bad dream." We both hoped to awaken, sweating and gasping for air, shards of terror clinging to our minds, until we realized that we were not asleep and this was no mere nightmare.

When Cecilia had mentioned to us that we could come back to hold Johnny after the harvesting of his organs, I had said, "We'd like that." I turned to Maureen and said, "You know I have to do this." She agreed. One of the hardest things for her was that from the time of the accident she had never been able to hold Johnny. He had gone from the ambulance to the hospital and had been wired up, in traction, and lying on the bed, unconscious. Every motherly instinct in her craved to hold him and comfort him, to take away the pain, to do anything to make it better. But she could not. To hold him one last time was a need eclipsed only by desire.

At 3:30 A.M. the phone rang. Cecilia said, "The operation is done. The organs are harvested. You can come now if you wish." "We'll be there in twenty minutes. By the way," I said, wanting to protect Maureen from any further trauma, "what should we expect when we see him?" "He'll be covered with a sheet and he'll have bandages over his eyes. And he'll be cold."

Silently and quickly we dressed, combed our hair, brushed our teeth. Silently we got in the car and drove to the emergency room. Cecilia met us there with two other nurses. We walked down the hallway holding hands, through a set of hospital double doors, into a large, empty room. We walked to the end of that room and into a smaller room. There, lying on a bed, eyes covered with bandages, was our beloved little boy. Small. Blond. Freckled. Cold. Dead. Immediately we reached out to touch, to embrace. There was nothing to do but weep. "Oh Johnny, Johnny, Johnny. We love you so much." I kissed his forehead. I brushed that impossible blond hair with my hand. Maureen reached for his lips and moved her hands up and down arms and legs so full of life a few short hours ago. We touched his torso but not too closely for fear of moving a bandage. The moment was excruciating, yet sacred. It was our personal Calvary. We were participating in the crucifixion. Only it was we who were being crucified. "Would you like to hold him?" one of the nurses asked. "Yes, let's give him to his mother." Maureen sat down and three of us picked him up and laid him in her arms. And there they were. Mother and son. Mary and Jesus. Maureen and John-Paul.

Some moments are so sacred that one dare not clothe them in anything but silence. I watched as Maureen held her dead child in her arms, and listened as she drew her child to her breast and touched his face with hers. "John-Paul, it was such a privilege to be your mother. It was such a privilege to carry you in my womb. I labored to give birth to you and when you were born I nursed you and fed you and loved you. It was such a privilege to watch you grow up. You were such a good boy, Johnny, and I love you so much, and we can't wait to see you again. Oh, Johnny, I'm so sorry this happened to you. I'm so sorry. Pray for us, Johnny." There she was, touching him, kissing him, stroking him.

Never was a poem written, a painting painted, a song sung that could touch that moment. Time stood still for this maternal lament coming from the deepest recesses of her mother's heart, broken, shattered, uncomprehending, yet filled with faith and love so strong that it knocked the very darkness clear across the room. Rocking her son in her arms as she had done a thousand times before.

It was my turn. "I can lift him," I said to the nurses, "I can lift him." How many times had I lifted him. Forty-eight hours ago I was throwing him up in the air at the pool. Yesterday at lunch we were playing freeze tag at the park. I can lift him. Every morning he had come into our bedroom and laid down on top of me. Every night he wanted to play "get on the floor and catch me." Every day at Mass with a perfectly unconscious elegance he would take my arm and drape it across his chest and hold his hand in mine. I can lift him.

So I picked him up—all fifty-eight pounds of him—and sat down and drew him to myself. And I wailed. My boy is dead. I wept and wept. I touched him and held him and talked to him. There was something urgent about wanting to hold in death this flesh I loved so much in life. There were no words to describe the pain. It was unimaginable, inconceivable, untouchable. I had always thought that the death of a child was the greatest cross a parent could be asked to bear. And here we were, staggering under its weight.

Yet, beneath the darkness that surrounded us, there it was: one glowing ember. Not yet near enough to give warmth; not yet bright enough to give light. But real. A reminder. And it spoke, saying, "I will carry you."

THREE

The Many Ways of Saying Good-bye

I am sitting at the cemetery with my brother-in-law J.J. We have an appointment to pick out a burial plot. J.J. is coming unglued. So am I. There was something in me, some latent power, that was almost hysterically opposed to the moment when I would put my son in a box, close the lid, put the box in the ground, and throw dirt on top of it. I was not showing it. But I felt like a tiger in a cage. I said to J.J., "I don't want to do this. What am I doing here looking at a burial plot for a six-year-old? I don't want to put him in a box, and I don't want to bury him in the ground." I felt a complete and total revulsion that was as much physiological as it was mental.

We made the necessary arrangements with the cemetery director, and I went home to help Maureen find clothes for Johnny to wear at the wake. We were in the closet, picking out slacks and shoes, tie and blazer. Maureen ironed a shirt for Johnny to wear. An actor in someone else's drama. Mothers do not spend their Wednesday mornings ironing shirts for their children to wear in caskets. J.J. came back. We forgot the socks and underwear. How would we know? We never dressed a corpse before.

Friends and family: They moved in and out with food, laundry, things the children would need to wear. They moved quietly and spoke quietly. They were part of the drama. They, too, were in disbelief. Words? Words were few because there were no words to say. It was as simple as that. But I will never forget their eyes: eyes that met mine and told me that I was not alone and that my family was not alone. Eyes that told me they felt our pain. Nor will I forget the embraces that offered a moment's respite, a place to lay some of the weight, the comfort that words could not give. In that moment, no words could help. So we talked about what needed to happen next.

J.J. is both friend and family. We met twenty years ago at a church service. He walked in, handsome as a movie star, wearing a brown leather jacket and a long scarf. He looked so good that I wondered what he was doing there. But when he sat down next to a young Down's syndrome boy and started playing with him, I knew there was something different about him: some wellspring, some mystery. J.J. was beginning a relationship with God after confronting much pain and brokenness in his own life. He was bright, talkative, and outgoing, a superb athlete and a particularly talented soccer player. There was, however, always something more to J.J.: something hidden, vulnerable, some unexpressed longing for a place to rest his soul.

We had both recently graduated from college. As we came to know each other we forged an extraordinarily deep friendship. I used to kid him, "You know, J.J., we would have become friends even if we had met years ago. You would have gone out with all your jock friends and talked about girls or sports, and I would have gone out with my arty, intellectual friends and talked about the symbolism of Bergman's latest movie. But at the end of the night we would have gone out together and had a better time with each other than we'd had with anybody else."

J.J. and I ended up moving to London together a year later to do evangelistic work. I still occasionally kid him about the fact that I never had to forgive or ask forgiveness of one individual so many times in one year. I am sure he could say the same. But as our trust of one another grew, we could tell one another about the things in our lives that did not work so well, or did not work at all. God's healing and strength came to us through each other. Twenty years later, I do not think there is anything important that we do not know about each other.

Two years after we moved to London, J.J. returned to New Jersey to marry Maureen's sister, Nancy. J.J. is now a very successful financial consultant in his mid-forties, the father of nine, a bit more stout, and his hair is thinning by degrees. As for our friendship, we can nearly look at each other and figure out what is going on. And we can get right down to business if something needs talking out.

When Johnny died, J.J. called his secretary and said, "Cancel my appointments for the rest of the week." He came with bagels in the morning. He came to hug the children and Maureen. He went to the bank and then handed me money, saying, "Here, you'll have expenses." He stood in the driveway and wept. Somehow, he had room in his heart for the endless pain in mine. J.J. was there with me like a sentinel at his post.

The shock numbed me enough to let me keep moving on to the next thing to be done. But it was regularly sliced open by a pain that made me want to scream. No, no, no, I wanted to scream from the deepest place within me. No, no, no, I wanted to scream all the way from heaven to hell. No. I wanted to protest unto death that this had happened. This is my son! I wanted to beat on God's breast like a deranged prize-fighter, but I was pounding less in anger than in pain, because I hurt too much to be angry. I was standing in the hallway greeting people and at the same time felt as though I was falling off a cliff. Then a voice or a touch would call me back. My daughter

Susanna was tugging at me. I must be there for her, I tell myself, but it was really she who was saving me.

Decisions mount. The casket—open or closed? We decided on an open casket so that everyone could see Johnny. Some thought this was a bad idea, that it would disturb people and traumatize the children. People unconsciously project their fear of death onto others. I thought just the opposite: It would be much worse for the children never to have seen Johnny again. Seeing him would bring the reality home. They needed to see the dead body to realize he was really dead and did not just disappear. It would take the terror away from death on the level of the imagination. It ought to; the reality is difficult enough. Say what you will about wanting to remember him full of life, happy, running around: we wanted as many last glances as we could get.

Others wondered if children should come to the wake. We said yes. It's closure. It's real. He's really dead. It's sad but not scary. It could be more scary to be left with only one's imagination, to wonder what happened, or how he looked. It would be different if he had been radically disfigured; Johnny's face was virtually untouched by the accident.

On the evening of the first wake we arrived at the funeral home a half hour early to spend time alone with Johnny. Then the doors opened. People kept coming and coming. Most we knew; some we did not. Some simply burst into tears. In a strange twist we found ourselves trying to comfort them. Others were close friends: We looked at each other and they were seared with our pain. There was nothing they could say except, "I'm sorry. I'm so sorry." I encouraged the children to come close to Johnny, to touch him and talk to him. His skin was cold.

I think many people saw their child in the coffin and could not believe this had actually happened. I knew how they felt.

I could not believe this had happened. An actor in someone else's drama. This happens to other families, tragic or heroic families. But not to us. We have never claimed those categories for ourselves.

It was exhausting to greet everyone. We had their grief to contend with as well as our own. And yet the outpouring of love was at the same time energizing. Scripture says that faith makes its power felt through love. There was a profound faith expressed all around us in countless gestures of love.

The funeral was the day after the second wake. The Christian community we belong to, the People of Hope, was taking care of the reception. School was canceled so the children could come to the funeral. The school choir would be singing. It was a hard day to think about. I knew I had to let it come and to keep yielding to facts that were no less awful for being true. The man who hit the boys came with his family to the wake. People were reaching out to him. I asked him to sit with us at the funeral. We had told him we forgave him. He was in deep pain. I cannot imagine his pain.

Finally we were able to go to bed. I woke up during the night, weeping. I did not wake up and then start weeping. I simply woke up with tears streaming down my face and sobs caught in my chest. Maureen heard me and woke up. How many times could we say, "Is this really happening? This can't be happening. This can't be happening. Is our son really dead?" Maureen placed her hand on my head and prayed, "Lord, give Gregory patience until he sees John-Paul again." It would prove to be the single most helpful prayer of all: patience, until I see you again, dear sweet boy.

After a fitful few hours, Maureen and I got up. We prayed with each other for the grace to surrender this day to the Lord. It was quiet in the house. We fed the children and dressed them. Then we drove to the funeral home for a last, private, family visit.

Johnny's casket had things in it, little things that his friends had made: things with crayons and bright ribbons, cards and drawings on paper plates and colored paper; things that will go into the earth with him until the resurrection of the dead. Little prayers, and little secrets. One or two that said, "Please don't open." And I did not. I wanted to, but I did not. I will wait until the end of the world to know what those little secrets were.

It was time to end. Time for the children to whisper into his ear one last wish, one last word of love. Time for one last glance, one last touch, one last kiss. Time we never could have imagined or conceived. They kissed him. We kissed him. We were ushered into another room while they closed the casket and placed it in the hearse.

And so the good-byes. The kisses, the touches, the ribbons, the tears. The quiet words. The time alone with him. The uncomprehending glances. The shirt ironed, the hair stroked. The deep things spoken in his ear. The crowd and the children, the silence and the music. The many ways of saying good-bye.

FOUR

A Mother's Arms

Late the previous night Father Philip Merdinger had sat with the two of us. Father Philip married us, baptized our first child, and has been one of our dearest friends since we were both young and single. He would be saying the funeral Mass. "Up to now, you've been carrying this," he said. "Tomorrow, Mother Church carries you." Because I trust him, I can lean on his words.

Mother Church. It is a curious phrase when one first hears it, since in the Roman Catholic tradition one pictures a Church largely governed by men. There is, however, a deeper poetry and deeper mystery. The Church is mother because she is wedded to Christ, one with him. As C.S. Lewis has said, "He is so masculine, that in relationship to him, everything else is feminine." Her motherhood has nothing to do with her innate perfection and everything to do with his choice of her. She is mother because she brings to birth in baptism all who call upon the name of the Lord; mother because she is in labor until Christ is born in all; mother because she gives flesh to the Word of God in her life of charity and service; mother because she loves her children, feeds them, teaches them, trains them, points out to them the way of life and death. She is mother because she protects them with all the power of her prayers and sacraments, and there is nothing as fierce as a mother's love.

The Church is mother because she is present at every step of the journey, holding in her heart all the hopes and dreams, fears and disappointments, sorrows, joys, and pain of the entire human family. She is receptive, attentive, listening. She is mother because she makes room in her heart for all the weary who need shelter from the storm and shade from the heat, for all those who need rest and have nowhere to lay their heads. Yes, she is mother. To let her carry us, shoulder this burden with us, was an inestimable grace.

For the funeral, we tried to choose Scripture readings that would reflect the human dimensions of this tragedy and set them against the horizon of hope which the death and resurrection of the Lord has forever set in human history. The Gospel reading was meant for John-Paul. The epistle was intended for the congregation. Father Philip's homily interpreted the readings beautifully.

Father Philip is an exceptionally gifted preacher. Because he is honest with God and with himself, he has considerable authority. He is also a man of great passion, like so many celibate figures throughout history. Added to these traits is his innate sense of drama: the drama of relationships, of marriage and celibacy; the drama of liturgy, the drama of grace breaking into our broken humanity. For this priest, these are all acts within the larger drama of the Incarnation, the Word of God becoming flesh and dwelling among us. He also has a resonant voice and an instinct for poetic phrasing. One can always expect a fresh and powerful sermon.

Several friends later told me that before the funeral began they saw Father Philip kneeling in prayer. They said he looked as if he were having a conversation with God. He was nodding his head, speaking words quietly, lending his ear as if to discuss with God what should be said and what should not, closing his eyes and asking for help.

After the Gospel reading, he walked over to the podium, paused, and looked at us. I knew that look well. It is one of compassion and truth. It bespeaks a serene acceptance of the fragile complexity of our already redeemed and not yet fully redeemed humanity. That look has penetrated my soul on countless occasions. In this moment, however, he was taking in the entire family in one long, extended glance.

I would like to reflect on the passages from Scripture and upon John-Paul's life in two ways. First of all, with regard to himself and then with regard to his parents, his family, and by extension, the rest of us.

The first part is about John-Paul. I would like to say this: He had it very good! He was a most fortunate young man. Look at the parents who gave him life. Look at his brothers and sisters. Of course they're not perfect. Neither was he; he was only six-and-a-half years old. Look at the community into which he was born, the People of Hope, one of the most profound expressions of the fostering and renewal of Catholic family life that I know. And that goes not only for the current members of the People of Hope, but for all of us who are here in the church today who have lived with the People of Hope, have ministered and have grown in the life of Christ in that community. There are a lot of us here who share the glory and the power of this expression of the renewal of Catholic family life, with all of its potential for this world and for the next.

Yes, John-Paul was a most fortunate young man. Look at the Church into which he was brought to baptism by his parents. The prayers he was taught. The songs he learned. The rituals of Mother Church that he was made a part of and assisted at. All of that, reaching out toward the full life of the human person. John-Paul had it good. And now, Mother

Church says to us that since John-Paul has not yet attained to the use of moral reason—he had not yet reached the usual age for First Confession and First Holy Communion—we can know with certainty that he has been received into heaven, received directly and immediately into eternal life.

Before he could draw his next breath, the most amazing thing happened. The congregation began to clap spontaneously, until the church was full of thunderous applause. Had it not been so perfect it would have been downright odd. This was, after all, Mass. But the congregation was honoring Christ himself, thanking him for the victory he won on Calvary, a victory that is nowhere more appreciated than in the stark corridors of death. For one brief moment, it seemed, the light of glory had broken through everyone's pain like sunlight on a cloudy, winter's day. Father Philip gestured toward the congregation and continued.

The second part has to do with his parents and family, and by extension, all of us. Here the statements are not quite as certain, the answers not as clear. Here the mystery of human life is deeper, harder to grasp. For us, on our side, we need to say that something very wrong has happened here, something that causes us tremendous grief and pain. And while compared to the events of this unhappy century this may not be the worst, nevertheless grief is grief and loss is loss and we need to deal with that. Not to do so would not be proper for a funeral homily. Even as we believe in the truth of the words of the funeral Mass: "The sadness of death gives way to immortality," we cannot leave too quickly the reality of the "sadness of death." There is something wrong with death, the unwilling separation of body and spirit.

May we be consoled by the reading from the letter to the Romans: "I consider that the sufferings of this present time are nothing compared with the glory to be revealed for us" [Romans 8:18]. As believing, committed Christians we cling to the promise of "glory to be revealed." But our humanity demands that we acknowledge "the sufferings of the present." In death the suffering is one of separation and loss, a separation and loss which brings anguish and grief. "How am I to live without him?" Maureen asked me. "How am I to live without him?" I don't know! There is the cause for grief: the separation. A separation from mother and father, from brothers and sisters, from us all. Our solace is Jesus; our hope and our comfort is Jesus. Jesus has conquered sin, which causes the "sting of death," namely, the eternal separation not only from each other but even from God. In Christ's victory over sin, and our participation in that through Baptism, is our victory over the "sting of death." In Jesus, the separation is only temporary, the loss only for a time. And so we take our stand this sad day in the victory of Jesus and say, "Salvation is stronger than sin; the new creation more powerful than the old!" If we are faithful to Jesus, if we repent of our sins and all that is un-Christlike in us, then we, too, will take on the "new man" which will ready us for eternal life. And so we turn to you, John-Paul, and say: "So long young man, so long, until we, too, see Jesus. And when we see Jesus, we will see you also, seated securely on his lap!"

For several moments no one stirred, not even the children. I was reminded of the line from Gerard Manley Hopkins's poem "God's Grandeur": ". . . the Holy Ghost over the bent world broods with warm breast and with ah! bright wings." That was what it felt like. Not a breath could be heard as God's word made its way into the minds and hearts of those present, giving relief to some, strength to others, and hope to all. After this pause, so full of the presence of God, the liturgy, with its solemnity and predictability, its majesty and grace, its ancient words and gestures, moved toward its climax.

After Communion I stood up. I had told Maureen earlier that I wanted to say something at the funeral. Her response was, "You?" For days I had not been able to speak two sentences in a row. "I'm going to write something," I said. "If God opens a door, I'll go through it." After receiving the Eucharist, I experienced a deep peace and the certainty that I could give what I called "A Father's Reflection." I walked past Johnny's casket, bowed before the altar, and made my way forward. I paused, took a deep breath, said a quick prayer, and looked at Maureen and the children.

When God decided to create John-Paul, he took the brightest colors in his paint box. And he made of our son a rainbow, a luminous splash of color to everyone he met. Just as a rainbow in all its beauty takes a shaft of sunlight and sends it through a dewdrop or raindrop, so God communicated his light to so many through John-Paul, and this light turned into the most marvelous array of colors. Johnny was our sunshine boy. He brought laughter and smiles, tangible excitement and almost incredible joy and happiness wherever he went. Often I would turn to Maureen and say, "I cannot believe how much I love that boy. Are all parents this nuts about their children?" Words cannot express the love that we shared with our son John-Paul.

Johnny was hit by a car on Monday. When Maureen and I got together later that night I said to her, "Honey, there's something I've never shared with you." And I told her that often, as I would reflect on our life together, I would pray,

"Lord, we have been so richly blessed—a marriage of such love and joy, unity and laughter." Then I'd think of the children: Gregory, Thérèse, David, John-Paul, Rose, Susanna, and Nicole—of the beautiful hearts and minds and personalities that God had given them. I would think how much I love them. And I would wonder if God would ever demand of me the ultimate sacrifice of giving one of them back to him. "Come on, Gregory," I would say to myself, "that's just your Irish personality." But the thought lingered, a distant minor chord in the music that was our family life.

Maureen spoke quietly: "Of all the children, John-Paul was the one who asked most about heaven. He wanted to know what it was like. He was concerned about whether he'd make it. About a week ago he said to me, 'Mom, do you think I'm going to go to heaven soon?' 'Well, John-Paul,' I said, 'I don't think so. Jesus has a time for each one of us, and we don't know what that time is, but he wants us to live each day as if he were coming to take us home.' It fills me with the most profound awe I have ever known to think that the Spirit of God was whispering into the soul of this precious little boy intimations about his imminent passage into eternal life."

John-Paul was killed right outside our front door. I have walked every day to the place of his accident. I kneel, I weep, I stare at the ground. The sorrow Maureen and I feel is the most profound experience of our lives. There are no words to describe it. But I have come to see that sorrow can go only as deep as love. And always, always, love is the ground beneath sorrow as well as the sky above it.

Yesterday when I walked out to the edge of the road I looked down at the ditch where he had lain. The sorrow and the tragedy of it all are unspeakable. As I knelt on the ground the words of the psalmist came to mind, "I will lift my eyes to the hills. From whence comes my help? My help comes from the LORD, who made heaven and earth" [Psalm 121:1–2 NKJV]. And I began to see that when I look to the earth I am filled with pain that I cannot bear—the horror is too great. But when I look to the hills, when I lift my gaze from earth to heaven, peace comes to my soul; a certain deep quiet comes over my mind. When I lift my eyes from the place where he lay to the place where he lives, I begin to hope. And my hope is this: that I shall see him again. Does hope replace pain? No. Hope does not replace pain. Hope embroiders pain and ultimately hope transcends pain. But the hope that Maureen and I share in the resurrection is far firmer than the ground we stand on today.

A final word. There is one Scripture that has consoled me this week. It is from the Gospel of John: "Standing by the cross of Jesus was his mother" [John 19:25]. I have kept turning to Mary this week. I say to her, "You know the pain. You are the only one around who knows what this feels like. You know the pain, the anguish, the grief. And you stood your ground. You didn't say a word because there are no words to say. But you stood and believed. You stood and trusted. You stood and hoped. And I will stand with you, silent. I will believe with you, trust with you, hope with you."

To our friends and family, thank you for sharing this week and this liturgy with us. If the grief has been unspeakable, so too the gestures of love, prayer, and support have gone way beyond what words are able to express. We pray that God will reward you for your kindness to us in a way befitting his glory. Let us pray with trust the mystery of our faith:

Dying you destroyed our death
Rising you restored our life
Lord Jesus, come in glory.

I sat down. Maureen's hand reached for mine. I had been able to do the thing I needed to do as the father of this family, to say something from us and for us. It was pure grace. I know, because it was the last time for ten weeks that I could put two sentences in a row.

Just before the end of Mass, Nora Coletta got up. She was Johnny's kindergarten teacher, and he was crazy about her. Johnny was the fourth of our children to have been in her class. The result was always the same. With high standards and immense creativity, Nora drew out of the children whatever was best in them. Nora has a tremendous presence, a great command of language, and a wonderful sense of humor. Beyond that, however, her only desire is that her little students know God's love and their own dignity as his sons and daughters. In her class, the children dance and sing and cook. They paint and play and act out the Scriptures. They learn to be kind to one another because she is so kind to them. When I had asked Maureen who should give the eulogy, she said, "Nora." "Yes," I said, "she's the one."

To those of you who don't know me, my name is Nora Coletta. I had the privilege, the delight, and the joy to be John-Paul's kindergarten teacher for the past eight months. Maureen and Gregory asked me to give this eulogy for John-Paul.

His parents tell me that he loved me. I loved him. I loved him very much and I still do love him. Anyone who knew John-Paul loved him. His greatest quality was love. He had a way of sneaking into everyone's heart, of snipping off a piece of it, and taking it with him. I know that is true, because a part of me went with him last Monday.

He loved his parents. He was so proud of his parents. He was so proud that Gregory and Maureen were his parents. He loved his brothers and sisters. He loved his grandparents, his aunts, his uncles, his cousins. He loved his friends and he loved his teachers. He loved little children especially. Even though he was little he loved children who were smaller than he was. He used to care for them by being kind and wanting to touch them. He was so excited when Nicole was born. He was so proud that he could hold Nicole for Mom while Mom took a shower.

Everything John-Paul did, he did with great zeal and with great enthusiasm. That's the way he prayed. He loved to pray. Sometimes in the classroom when we would pray, the teachers would get such delight that we would make eyes at each other because John-Paul would be there. His neck would be red and his face would be red. He would be praising the Lord and singing out loud and we would get such delight out of watching him pray.

Nora smiled, relishing the thought.

Right before Christmas, during Advent, the children had good deeds that we would try to do every day. One particular day the good deed was to place their hand upon Mom and say a prayer for her. When they got home from school, they were to pray over Mom. I explained to the children that Mom was very tired. It was before Christmas and she was doing a lot, and she needed prayer, and she would so appreciate it if they went home and put their little hands on her and prayed over her. As I was finishing my little speech, John-Paul started to get a very worried look on his face. He raised his hand and said, "Mrs. Coletta, Mrs. Coletta," and I said, "Yes, John-Paul," and he said, "What about you, who's going to pray over you? You're tired, you're busy . . . ." And before I could reassure him that somebody would pray over me, he said, "Well, what about us, can we come up and pray over you?" I said, "Sure!" He ran and got a little stool and I sat down on it and the children came up and prayed over me, and John-Paul led the prayer. He prayed that I would have peace, that I would have joy, and that I would have the strength to do all that I had to do for the busy Christmas season.

In our kindergarten class we are great intercessors and we have prayed for many people, and the children love to do that. We were praying for our friend, Mary Ann. She had some medical problems and she was going for a test, and we really needed that test to come out with good results, and so we prayed one day for Mary Ann. The next day one of the teacher's aides came in to tell me that Mary Ann's tests came out fine. As soon as I told the children that, John-Paul jumped out of his seat and said, "YES!" He did that when anything exciting happened; he'd say "YES!" He always prayed for those who were suffering from pain and sickness and for all the children of the world who had nothing to eat. Every day he prayed like that. John-Paul was holy and he thought it was cool to be holy and he wanted everybody to be holy.

John-Paul deferred. He would think nothing of wanting to be last in line, so that everybody could go before him. I know he deferred to his brothers and sisters at home. If I had a snack in the classroom or a special treat to be given out to everyone and there would be some left, maybe some of the children would ask me if they could have more and I'd count out what the snack was, and I would say, "Well not really, because I don't have enough for everyone else." Inevitably, John-Paul would say, "Well then don't give me any, give it to everybody else; if there isn't enough, you don't have to give me any."

His mom told me that if he didn't like what was being cooked for dinner he would offer to fast. He would tell her, "I thought this would be a good fast day."

John-Paul was so proud of his name. He was so proud that he was named after the Pope. One day I asked the kindergarten boys if any of them wanted to be a priest. Of course, in the kindergarten every hand goes up. Yet John-Paul's hand didn't go up. So I said, "John-Paul, what do you want to be if you don't want to be a priest?" He said, "I want to be Pope!" He wanted to bypass the whole priest thing. When we prayed for the Pope he prayed for "Pope Me."

He loved the fact that he was named John, after the disciple that Jesus loved so much. When I read Bible stories to the children, he couldn't wait until I got to the part about John. His face would light up because he knew that was his name.

John-Paul was the leader of our class, and he was a good leader. He set a good example for the children. We did so many extra things because John-Paul was there. He would want to act out the Bible stories and he would bug me until we did it. He would want to act out the stations of the cross and we did that. Every time when we did a story or Bible story and acted it out, he always wanted to be Jesus. He wanted to square dance. I don't know, it bugged me that he wanted to square dance. Over Easter vacation I was thinking about how we were going to do this, because I knew when I got back John-Paul was going to say, "When are we going to square dance?"

All the children always wanted to sit next to John-Paul, and they would argue when we would run over to the rug; everybody would want to sit next to him. He would get annoyed with that. After a while he would say, "Mrs. Coletta, why do they do that to me?" I'd say, "John-Paul, it's because they love you so much."

He was all boy, and he loved to play. He had a wonderful imagination. He loved to play outside. He loved to play with his brother David, with their GI Joe guys, and had a great time doing that. He loved to eat. He loved bagels with cream cheese, cookies, nachos, candy, and pizza. Last weekend his grand-mother took him for bagels with cream cheese. When the Floyds lived in Ireland, he and David would help the Sisters of Mercy do small jobs, always with an ulterior motive, because the reward was cookies. The last meal that he had was nachos and candy. So God took care of even the smallest details for John-Paul.

John-Paul wasn't afraid to die. In our kindergarten class we had many discussions about death and about heaven, and he knew death wasn't the end. He knew it was a change and it was a beginning. Most of those conversations were initiated by John-Paul. He had a tremendous excitement about heaven. He was excited to go to heaven. He had asked Maureen several times recently about death and wondered if he would die soon and did she think he would go to heaven? So God was prepar-ing him and God was preparing us also.

I told Gregory and Maureen a few months ago that John-Paul was very, very special and I thought that God had great plans for him. Little did I know how great those plans were. The plan that God had for John-Paul was instant sainthood.

Heaven is like a magnet; it draws the heavenly to it. Since Monday, I have had a verse in my mind which I would like to share with you. It's from 1 Corinthians 2:9: "Eye has not seen, ear has not heard, nor has it so much as dawned on man what God has prepared for those who love him."

Do you know what John-Paul would say to that?
"YES!"

The funeral liturgy, with its balance of grief and hope, drew to a close.

We drove to the cemetery where, with the ancient prayers of the Church, Johnny's body was committed to the earth. I thought this would be the moment I might not get through.

But as husband and father I knew I needed to lead Maureen and the children through this last hurdle of the week. I was governor, provider, protector—not easy roles when everything inside is breaking apart. Nonetheless, the roles were a grace given. They were a call imposed, a duty required. And mercifully, that grace enabled me, and us, to keep walking one step at a time.

Mother Church took John-Paul from his mother and father, sisters and brothers, and laid him in the earth. Without a word and with arms wide enough to reach around the entire family, she gathered us in and pressed us softly against her breast.

FIVE

The First Month

One day we went for a swim. It had been three weeks since we had gone swimming, and then we had been nine. The gap left by Johnny seemed much bigger than one. Still, there were six other children to care for. I realized I could not simply wall myself in and live, isolated, in my world of pain, much as I wanted to. Oh, how I wanted to. Left to myself I would close the doors, pull down the shades, and sit in the darkness because there was only one word that described my world: pain. But I could not wall myself off. So I took the kids swimming.

It was Mother's Day. In our family we have a tradition: The children take time to honor their mother on Mother's Day, particularly to thank her for giving them life. What would they say today? They could talk so freely. I could not talk yet. Maureen and I spoke with our eyes and our touch. But words did not work yet, at least not for anything other than the everyday business of picking up milk or dropping off kids or going to the library. Anything deeper stuck in my throat.

The children sat with her at the kitchen table. They told her how much they love her and how much she loves them, how she makes them lunch and helps them with their homework, plays with them and reads them stories. They adore their mother. They kissed her and touched her and smiled their irresistible smiles. I watched them with her. I saw her sorrow and her pain. But in this moment what shone most brightly was her mother's heart.

I could use many words to describe Maureen: wife, friend, lover, companion, advisor. But she takes the word "mother" and charges it with the strength, authority, and dignity it has always had when cultures are thriving. She is one with the countless women, known and unknown, for whom mothering has always been a gift and a challenge, something that is both a treasure and an art. Motherhood was something received in her very biological and psychological makeup as well as something to be formed, explored, and cultivated. For Maureen, being a mother is a status that needs no other adjectives around it to shore it up or lend it prominence. She lives her role with the confidence and security of one who knows she's exactly where she should be. I do not mean to imply for a minute that her gifts are limited to or circumscribed by the care of the children. She has gifts that go well beyond what the children need. But for her, for now, being a mother is the context for all her other thoughts and dreams.

Her mothering comes from a deep reservoir. She can give of herself generously. Even in this season of exhaustion and heartbreak, there she was: nursing the baby, coloring with the girls, doing homework, taking Thérèse out, sitting at the table talking with the boys. Somehow she was in on the secret of how to receive God's love. God is her hope, her strength, her joy, her first and greatest love. She believes in him and trusts him. Because of this, she knows who she is. And while she derives a certain mystical, prophetic, and visionary angle from something latent in her Irish blood, she is also blessed with the stability and deep interior stillness that come from her German and Polish ancestors. She knows how to suffer well.

Maureen and I are good for each other. I tell her that with our different gifts, backgrounds, and limitations, we keep pulling each other to the center where Christ is: "the still point of the turning world," as T.S. Eliot says. Naturally, whenever one of the children does something particularly exaggerated or dramatic, I look at her and say, "There they go again, with those Helfrich genes!"

Is she perfect? Far from it. At times she loses her perspective, reaches the end of her rope, tells me she cannot take any more. But she is beyond my wildest hopes and dreams as mother to our children. On this Mother's Day she was a bereaved mother, a mother of sorrows, loving the ones who were at the table and aching for the one who was gone, with a pain only a mother could know.

Later in the day, Mark and Nancy (my brother and sister-in-law) invited us to a family picnic. Typical of everything they had done for us, Nancy said, "No pressure. Drop in if you feel like it. We want to do what's easiest for you and we don't know what to do or what works best." We did not know either, so we went. People wanted to reach out and draw us into the conversation of everyday life. But I could not yet enter that conversation. People were passing pasta and talking about vacations and I could hardly breathe.

At one point I went out for a walk with Susanna. I cried out to God, "Three weeks ago I was swimming with that boy. Three weeks ago I saw that beautiful little body so full of life and joy and love. Three weeks ago I held him in my arms, stood him on my shoulders, threw him in the air, and dived through the water with him. Three weeks ago. Oh God, how can this be?" It could not be but it was. It violated every notion of what is right and normal. It violated every casually uttered comment I ever heard or made about God as Father or about angels who watch over children. Every childhood picture deep in the subconscious was torn asunder by the shock of it all. The guardian angels help the children over the rickety bridge in that Hummel-like painting. But here they had moved neither car nor boy.

Does the world over which God reigns really work like this? Do angels really step in and intervene? Or are these simply remnants of childhood faith, so needed that they are kept, so cherished that they are held onto until they are broken on the broken body of a child?

We were said to be grieving. What is this word "grief"? It is from the Latin *gravare:* to burden. The dictionary says: "a deep and poignant distress caused by bereavement." Unpacking that line is like reading free-form verse:

Grief
extending
far downward from the top
inward from the surface
coming from far down
extreme
strongly felt
dark and rich
sunk in
absorbed by
intense
darkest or most
silent
piercing
stinging
making a hole
harm

sharp

injury

loss

like a needle

severe

acute

leading to culmination or

breaking point

extreme uneasiness of mind

abnormal

overwhelming

from the Middle English *bereven:* to

rob

plunder

deprive

strip

leave destitute

The English language does a good job describing aspects of grief. Burden? Yes. Heavy? Yes. Extending far downward or inward? Yes. Dark and hard to understand? Undoubtedly. Extreme and intense, piercing; leaving a hole? Absolutely. Like a needle, sharp and stinging? Yes. Extreme form of mental pain that makes its presence felt in the physical body? Yes. Uneasiness of mind? No. Grief is much more than an uneasiness. And bereaved, that's the best definition of all: robbed, plundered, deprived, stripped. At 3:19 P.M., laughing; at 3:20 P.M., dead.

The morning after Mother's Day we were lying in bed. It was about 6:30. "I'm going to get up," I said. "I need a hug," was Maureen's reply. So I gave her a hug and then lay back on the bed for a minute. "I'm going to get up," I said, and she turned to lean her head on my chest. And there we lay.

40

And her hand began to move ever so slowly, ever so lightly, haltingly, questioning, neither of us quite sure. Slowly, silently, tenderly, we made love for the first time since the accident. Heart to heart, flesh to flesh, deep calling to deep. For better or worse, in joy and in pain, as close as possible—Maureen offering this moment to me to remind me that there is more to reality than just the death of John-Paul. Our embrace was a profound, extended moment of intimacy and grace: grace to carry on, to bear the burden, to surrender to God in the unbearable mystery of his having allowed this, knowing that he is with us not to remove suffering but to redeem it. It was the grace to know that God is with us and suffers with us, that he loves us in our suffering and not simply to get us beyond it. It was the grace of this sacred moment that brought peace and healing to our battered souls. Indeed, life is not only about Johnny's death.

Who is this woman who shares my soul, my life, my bed? We went out to dinner that night, just the two of us and the baby. As we ate I asked her, "How are you doing with your husband?" "I think you're doing a little better in the last few days. But there were times over the last few weeks when I felt like I couldn't reach you; I couldn't even get to where you were. All I could do was offer you to God and say, 'Father, you have to console him.'"

How true this was. We could not even console each other. Such was the overwhelming grief we felt that we could not even console our dearest friend. This was almost cruel. In the normal course of life's peaks and valleys I am there for her and she for me. But this was terrain we did not know, a forest so dense that we lost our sense of direction. We were quite literally bewildered—lost in a wilderness with no recognizable landmarks. Except for one thing: We knew we were

41

not alone. The God of Jesus Christ, who spoke not a word because he knows we could not hear one, was with us like the air we breathe: a vast presence, subtle but nonetheless so real and firm. We did not need him to say anything. We needed him just to hold us, to hear our heart break again and again, to tell him how unbearable this was and that if he did not shoulder the burden we would be lost. He was always there. The psalmist says: " . . . I am always with you; you take hold of my right hand" (Psalm 73:23). Touch was what was needed, not words. Yes, hold my right hand, and my left one, too. Hold my arms and my chest and most of all my head. Let it nestle in the crook of your neck, O great God, like Johnny's used to nestle in mine.

Maureen and I discovered a few things we could do: speak the truth in love, show one another affection, and give one another space to grieve. We could say to one another: We will see him again. This did nothing to ease the emotional pain, but it did enable us to fix God's truth in our minds. The pain wracked us, convulsed us, made us wonder whether we were capable of any more. Yet, just when we felt that we could not stand another minute, God breathed his word into our souls: "God is faithful and will not let you be tried beyond your strength; but with the trial he will also provide a way out, so that you may be able to bear it" (1 Corinthians 10:13).

One month passed. The mind does funny things in the midst of grief, as though one is living in a time warp. Sometimes the tragedy felt like three months ago and sometimes, three days. The emotional intensity felt like years. After one month the wound was fresh, open, and bleeding. Maureen and I could make it through one short, usually humorous line about Johnny, or one imaginative scenario with the children about heaven and what Johnny's doing there. But when we tried to talk to one another, we usually ended up looking out the window or down into our coffee. We were growing comfortable with each other's pain. We had radically given each other permission to let the moment be as painful as it was.

After Maureen and the children went to bed, I read a pile of cards that Gregory's classmates had sent to us. One of them said, "It must be awful." Yes it was awful. It was not awful that Johnny was in heaven. It was awful that he was not on earth. There was a number I kept counting when we went places, a name I kept calling out. There was a hole at the dinner table, an extra space in the car, too many bagels on Sunday morning. It was all this and more, including the recognition that virtually no one could understand this except another bereaved parent. God is a bereaved parent, however, and therein lay my hope.

The pain was relentless and terrible and isolating. It also made for a remarkable solidarity. It linked us with Rwanda and Ethiopia and Haiti—all the places Johnny used to pray for every night. I thought to myself, "I know you, Rwanda. I know you, Ethiopia and Haiti. We have wept with you on the news. We have prayed for you with our children. But now we share your pain as a stark reality. Your children were killed. Our child was killed. The geography, language, religion, and culture make no difference. I look in your eyes and I see myself, whether those eyes look at me from Times Square or Tiananmen Square. We both know something terrible has happened."

I was sitting with Gregory and David after family prayer. I said, "It's four weeks since Johnny was hit. How are you? Do you miss him?" David said, "I miss him." I asked, "How much do you miss him?" "As much as the whole world." I said, "I miss him too." Then I asked Gregory, "What do you miss about him?" He said, "Everything." I looked back over at David. Those beautiful blue eyes were brimming with tears.

"Come here," I said, and he climbed on my lap. Then this seven-year-old boy buried his head in my arms and wept for a half hour. The two of us wept. I motioned to Gregory. He came over and the three of us met in a father-son embrace that carried more love and sorrow than these tender years should hold. I thought my heart could not break any more until a moment like this arrived.

Thérèse had not said much yet. She was eight, the oldest girl, and therefore in some ways a helper, a little mother. She was asked to do a lot, as are the oldest children in any large family. But she also loves to do a lot—not the diapers and dishes and cleaning-her-room type of work. No, Thérèse loves to play with the girls, dressing them up in Maureen's old clothes and outrageous remnants from thrift shops. She loves to fix their hair and paint flowers on their nails. She loves to hold the babies and care for them. She loves to make people feel special and has an immense capacity to give of herself if she is motivated. There is nothing learned or practiced in this. It is all as natural as a sunflower growing tall. To see her with her younger sisters (in her good moments, which most of her moments are!) is to see a totally instinctive, unrehearsed, femininity coming into bloom.

There is also much in her that comes from me. She loves to tell the story about the time we were having nachos for dinner. There was nothing left on the plate but plain tortilla chips. She and I were making the best of the situation when Gregory came by with a fresh plate loaded with melted cheddar. We both threw back our plain chips and reached for the new ones at exactly the same moment. We looked at each other and dissolved in a fit of laughter, two thieves caught in the act. To this day we laugh about it. She knows there are parts of her I can read like a book because it is like reading my autobiography. We love each other dearly and drive each other crazy.

Thérèse had been the third one out the door on that awful day. When she had not been able to sit inside any longer she had run outside and found her brothers unconscious. She saw them taken away in the ambulances, sirens wailing. She has realized, in retrospect, that she was looking at her dead brother on the lawn. Thérèse has a vivid imagination, and I am sure these images are carved in her soul. She prayed in family prayer that Jesus "would take away all this grief from our family." In a moment of anger she blurted out, "I hate all this grief!" Johnny's death was a fierce interruption to her happy world. I knew we had much to talk about that she could not yet even voice.

Jesus prayed in the Garden of Gethsemane: "My soul is sorrowful even to death" (Matthew 26:38). This was how I felt one month after John-Paul's death: sorrowful unto death. Part of me wished I could die so the pain would end, because living through this was such agony. I was back at work, the flowers had died, the mail had subsided, and the fruit baskets had stopped arriving. I had a wife and six other children to care for. There were birthdays, First Communions, and graduations, and I would not deny any of these celebrations to the children. Maureen and I moved through them, but then we would turn a corner and seemingly out of nowhere, with no advance preparation, we would get smacked. The pain was like a bird caught inside a room, smashing itself against the window, trying to get free, and not understanding why it cannot get through the pane of glass. My soul beat against my body, trying to move somewhere with the pain. At times I felt I could tear my skin off.

I understand with a newfound sympathy why people become drug addicts and alcoholics after the death of a child. I understand why marriages break up. I said to Maureen, "If it's this hard with the Lord, can you imagine what it's like without him?" Devastation is a light turn of phrase. For Maureen and me, all we could do was embrace the cross, wrap our arms around it, and hang on for dear life, willing to understand nothing. But without the cross and the hope that it promises, I can understand why people head for the nearest bar, drugstore, or drug dealer. One must do something with the pain.

One month. There were times when I felt I could breathe, and times when grief seemed to take my breath away, times when I would be buying cheese or ketchup or light bulbs and I would look at life going on around me and I would say to myself, "My son has died. I can't just buy light bulbs, or go to the dry cleaner's, or mow the lawn. My son is dead."

I started writing a song to Christ while I was walking along the beach with Nicole in a carrier on my back:

> All I can give you is my pain,
> I have nothing else to give.
> I give it all to you
> And never reach the end.

A month later, and we were still confronted with the dreadful reality: How will we make it through? I was unafraid to ask the question, because I knew that the pierced hand of Christ would guide us.

Maureen and I were learning that we grieve differently from the children. I think that God drew a veil over part of the children's minds and emotions because he did not want them to suffer beyond their ability to cope. This is not to say they did not grieve, but rather to say they grieved as children and siblings, and not as parents. It was a different kind of grief. I was sure he would pull back that veil a bit at a time as they became able to let more in.

Shortly after Johnny's death Maureen said to me, "I feel afraid that this is going to happen again." I said to her, "I can't believe you're saying that. I have been feeling the same thing." It must be a kind of psychological aftershock, like the tremors that follow an earthquake. I prayed to the Lord, "One is enough. Can you please assure me that nothing like this will ever happen again?" Of course God makes no such assurances. Later in the conversation, Maureen said to me, "Our love for God has to be greater than our love for John-Paul, and the only way we can express that is to trust him. Only faith can say to grief, 'This, too, shall pass.'" We were trying to live honestly with one another, and the truth we both realized intuitively was that grief is not something to be wrapped up and put on the shelf a few days after the funeral. A week after the burial I said to Maureen, "He's not buried a week. It can't be a week since we buried our boy."

I remember taking Maureen's hand and walking to the place where he was hit, one week after the accident. We stood there, trying to pray, feeling as though we could sink through the earth. I looked up and saw a car. It was 3:20 P.M., the same time Johnny was hit, and a car was coming toward us. I could hardly believe my eyes. I kept imaging Johnny and David. The car stopped right in front of us. Out climbed Paul and Mary Alice Giegerich. Mary Alice had taken home ironing and was returning it. They came over and embraced us. "It happened here," I began, faltering. "Just a week ago. Right here," I said, pointing to the ground. "Paul," I cried, my voice cracking, "he was alive a week ago and now he's dead." I was trying to talk but I could not find my breath and I could not find the words. The four of us stood in the driveway, weeping.

The first few weeks were like that: pain like fire, pain like swords, pain I had to consciously turn away from because it was like a monster waiting to devour me. Yet, turn as I would, it was inside me and turned with me. It only slept when I did, yet seemed to sleep with one eye open, waiting for any sign of movement. As the weeks turned into a month, Maureen stood at the kitchen window, looking outward. "I still expect him to come running up the driveway," she said. "Then he doesn't, and this indescribable heaviness comes over me."

Last night was the "month's mind." Month's mind is a tradition we discovered when we lived in Ireland, where family and friends gather to pray one month after the death of a loved one. Since I had spoken at the funeral, I asked Maureen if she would like to say something to our friends and family who had gathered. Protesting that she had neither the time nor energy to prepare, she nonetheless agreed to speak.

Gregory and I would like to thank you all for coming tonight to this memorial for John-Paul.

At the funeral, Gregory shared a father's reflection, and I would like to share a brief, motherly reflection on the life of our son John-Paul—a bit more scattered than my husband, perhaps because of the care of our other six children, and the two babies in particular. But so many of you have asked how we are, and we'd like in some way to share that with you.

Our life is changed without our John-Paul, and the grief that we experience daily is so very deep. Our faith is a sure strength, but we miss him terribly, because we loved him so much. John-Paul was so very full of life. He was enthusiastic about everything he did or said. As Johnny's mother, I remember carrying him in my womb through a very long, hot summer, and laboring to bring him to birth, nursing him and nurturing him, correcting him, teaching him, and loving him. Four weeks ago, I held his lifeless body in my arms and told him what a privilege it was to be his mother. The line from Psalm 73, "I am always with you," reminds me of John-Paul. Johnny was always with me, and so the grief of his loss is a daily reality, and it feels like a constant one. I walk around the house and he seems to be everywhere. I think he'll come running up the stairs—Johnny never walked anywhere—and ask, "What's for dinner?" I've often gone, in the last month, to make his lunch at ten minutes to eleven, the time he would eat before he left for school.

His absence at our home and in our hearts is very big, and as his mother, I have to say, my own heart is broken. The grief and sorrow seem to tinge, if not fully color, everything at this early stage of loss. Just today, I took the children to do some errands, and I treated them to lunch. There was an extra seat at the table; and the bill seemed too small. On the way home we stopped at the graveyard and it seemed somehow unfair that Johnny's body lay there in the ground, that he was not eating ice cream with us in the van on the way home. If I could have my way, I'd love to have my Johnny back. And yet, as Christians, I cannot, and we cannot, stop at grief and mourning as though that were the end of the story. In 1 Corinthians 15, a verse that has been with me constantly, St. Paul says, "If for this life only we have hoped in Christ we are of all men the most to be pitied." If my faith and hope in Christ is only to have a good life here, then I am to be pitied. My hope needs to be in Christ for our life to come.

When I sit and feebly attempt to think and to pray, I can only see Johnny happy. I can only see John-Paul playing beneath the legs of the Lord, or riding piggyback, and yes, knowing John, organizing everything in heaven, perhaps even introducing Saint Francis to nachos.

I ran into a high school friend this week who lives locally, and had heard about the accident. She said to me, "You know,

Maureen, when a child dies this young I bet it's so hard—that you'll always think of what he was to become." But I know, and we know, that Johnny's greatest agony would be to return. He is perfectly happy. John-Paul is alive in Christ! He is perfectly whole! He is like God. Whatever Johnny could have become—a scientist, or a doctor—would pale tremendously to what he is now: perfectly whole, beholding the face of his Father.

A year ago John-Paul said to me, when things were going his own way, "Mom, you are the best Mom in the whole world, except of course for Mary." I was struck by his love for me, as well as his realization of a profound spiritual truth. He said it again and again—usually when he got a bagel or candy, but as I was praying and crying and crying and praying this week, I said, "John-Paul, say something to me, because I need to hear your voice." Johnny said to me once again, "Mom, I love you, and you're still the best Mom in the whole world, except for Mary, and she's here with me now, and I'm *very* happy."

Our fondest hope for all our children is that they would love God first, that they would grow up knowing how to love and give of themselves to others, and that one day they would achieve heaven. John-Paul has fulfilled our desires for him, and he has become everything that we could hope for. We have confident hope that John-Paul is in heaven, and our hearts rejoice that he is with God. And hasn't all of what's happened awakened us all to what's really important in life? We have seen God's glory, in the midst of this tragedy.

Finally, if the grief has been overwhelming, so, too, have been the love and prayers, the acts of kindness, and the thoughtfulness that we've experienced, literally from around the world. You've shared our grief and sorrow, and we experience so much love, that at times I'm at a loss to receive it all. I'm embarrassed at the wealth of all that we've been blessed with. I've had seven babies, and after labor and delivery, one of the things that I always look forward to are the blankets that the nurses warm in the incubators, and then place on my body. You've been like that for us, to stop the shaking and the chills, and all we can say is thank you. Thank you for being there for us, for loving us, for comforting us. You all mean so very much to us. You have exemplified for us the Body of Christ.

Please continue to pray for us, that God's grace will bear us up, and we will be able to embrace this cross each day. As we go forward, which we must, may we remember John-Paul as loving God and bringing happiness to all he met, and may his death change our lives and make us realize how necessary it is to live for Jesus Christ each day. We thank you and we love you.

At the end of the evening I saw something different on people's faces. I can only call it a look of relief. They heard in Maureen's words real faith, real hope, and real struggle. She showed no heroic high jinks, no false piety. She was just a mother talking about her love and her pain. Deep inside, they knew from these words that Maureen would make it to the other side of grief.

It was a fine evening, full of the warmth and love and affection of family and friends. David, who was seven, read the passage from 1 Corinthians 2:9: "Eye has not seen, ear has not heard, nor has it so much as dawned on the mind of man what God has in mind for those who love him." He did a great job with the reading.

But the following day was brutal. I did not know it was going to be like this: a cycle of darks and lights, highs and lows, moments of consolation followed by violent upheaval. Grief is like that—it sneaks up behind when we are not looking and then slams us across the back of our heads.

It is striking how the Scriptures come alive depending upon how much I need them. I am often neither spiritually awake enough to have them slice me open or desperate enough to have them heal me. But at that moment the word of God was writ large and bright on the walls of my mind. Earlier that week I had read from John's Gospel: "But I will see you again, and your hearts will rejoice, and no one will take your joy away from you" (John 16:22). I could hear Johnny saying, "Dad, I will see you again." God's word brings hope. At another moment I read from Job: "Woe to me if I am guilty; if I am innocent I dare not lift my head, so wholly abject, so drunk with pain am I" (Job 10:15 JB). So drunk with pain: This describes it well. I felt like an alcoholic, except I was drunk with grief. When I would think about living the rest of my life without John-Paul, of never seeing him again, the thought was unbearable. But when I would ask myself, "Can you make it through just today without him? Can you make it from morning until evening?" I would think, "Yes, I can." One day at a time, I could handle. One day at a time was all there is grace for. I had hope for tomorrow, but grace only for today.

Many things precipitated this weight of grief. One morning I took Gregory and David to the Cub Scout breakfast. I saw the boys with their dads and, before I could catch myself, thought, "You're here with all your sons, but one of my sons is dead." I clenched my teeth to get through the festivities. Then someone announced that David had won second prize for the Pinewood Derby. Instant flashback. All I could see was Johnny's face, laughing and smiling, so excited to see his brother winning that morning. I went outside, walking up and down the parking lot, trying to regain my equilibrium. J.J., who was there with his boys, saw me and said, "Come on, let's take a walk." We walked to the end of the school property. I leaned my head against the fence and wept. He stood there, head against my back, praying quietly, not trying to wish the moment away or move it somewhere else. He has an extraordinary ability to simply let the moment be what it is.

That evening at dinner Maureen and I decided we would read to the children the letter we had received from the Sharing Network, New Jersey's organ and tissue donor/recipient organization. The letter was about all the people who had received Johnny's organs. I often had wondered who had received Johnny's eyes. Johnny had the most beautiful eyes—eyes that sparkled and danced, eyes sso full of love and joy. I imagined meeting the people who have his eyes and wondered if I would recognize them.

During the meal, I took the letter and opened it—and could not read it. Maureen said, "Do you want me to read it?" And then the most remarkable thing happened. David left his chair and came over to me and sat on my lap. And then Gregory went over to Maureen and put his arm around her as she continued to read. But she, too, had to stop. So Thérèse picked up the letter and finished it, while the boys stood by their parents.

May 17, 1995

Dear Gregory and Maureen,

On behalf of the New Jersey Organ and Tissue Sharing Network, we would like to extend our deepest condolences on the loss of your son, John-Paul. The sudden and unexpected death of a loved one, especially a child, is surely one of the most painful events a family can endure. In this time of deep sadness you were able to give the most precious gift of all, the gift of life. How lucky for John-Paul that in his short lifetime he had the support and love of such parents as yourselves.

John-Paul's liver went to a 42-year-old New Jersey resident who had been diagnosed with end-stage liver disease. He is the father of two small children and the eldest is a nine-year-old little girl who is counting the days till her daddy can play with her again. The left kidney went to a 32-year-old New Jersey Transit worker who had been on dialysis for three years before this transplant. The right kidney went to a 45-year-old diabetic woman who is looking forward to getting back to work in her local elementary school as the librarian. This recipient had been waiting for two years while on dialysis. The heart was recovered and the valves will be transplanted at a later date. One of the corneas went to a six-month-old baby from Florida who was born blind. The second cornea went to a 29-year-old man from New York City who had been blind since an accident in college.

The value of the gifts you have given these families is immeasurable. We thank you on their behalf and hope that you find some measure of comfort in the months and years to come in the knowledge that you gave unselfishly and have had such a positive impact on the lives of others. John-Paul's spirit will go on, through the recipients, in every person they touch throughout their lives.

> With deepest respect,
> Cecilia W. David, R.N., M.S.N.
> Transplant Coordinator

When Thérèse had finished, David turned and asked, "Dad, can we talk about Johnny tonight?"

SIX

The Children and Grief

The children had lost a brother, a playmate, a friend. People wanted to know how they were doing. The question was asked in sympathy and utter sincerity. But the children were not a flock, like sheep, or a herd, like cattle. They were a group of unique and unrepeatable individuals. They were all faring differently and they were processing this tragic event at different times and in different ways. Their grief was as unique as they are. No neat, crisp, generic answer could be given. This much was true for all of them: They experienced the death of their brother profoundly.

Johnny had been dead five weeks. I was concerned about Gregory. He is intelligent and perceptive. Whenever he sensed that Maureen or I was having a hard time, he came up to us and stood beside us, put his arm around us, or rubbed our backs. This was remarkable behavior for a ten-year-old. He was trying to take care of us. This behavior, new since the accident, was his way of telling us he knew something. While the gesture was both kind and noble, we could not let him assume that role. That is not a young child's role. Our normally exuberant boy had been quiet at home, not as carefree and spontaneous as before. He was more moody and emotional. When I asked him how he was doing with Johnny's death he said, "I don't know. I can't explain it."

On a warm, beautiful, late spring evening the two of us spent some time together sitting in the family room. I mentioned my concern that all he said was "I can't explain it" in regard to his feelings about Johnny's death. "I have two ideas that I think might help," I said. "If you'd like, we can pray and ask God to help you put words on your experience of John-Paul's death. Then I thought you could write two stories: one on the death of John-Paul and one on the life of John-Paul. But for starters, is there anything you want to tell me about Johnny's death?"

Our ten-year-old replied, "I feel like I don't have as much sorrow for Johnny's death as I should. I mean, I miss him and I cried at the funeral and I cried at the memorial Mass, but when I see you and Mom and your sorrow, I feel. . . ." "A little guilty?" I asked. "Yes, like I should have more sorrow than I do."

"Son," I said, "you don't have to feel the sorrow Mom and Dad are feeling. In fact, God wouldn't want you to feel that kind of sorrow. God gives you a sorrow that is the right size and shape for a brother. That's different from the sorrow a mother or father feels. You don't need to feel what Mom and Dad are feeling. That's for parents. You've got your own sorrow that's more than enough for you."

The truth shall set you free. I could see that a burden he had been carrying for weeks was lifted. "Son, I know how much you loved Johnny. Think about all the love, laughter, and fun you had together. Remember this, and remember also how real and true your love for him was." I prayed with him, "Lord Jesus, help Gregory realize that you know how much he loved Johnny. Help him to see clearly how much *he* loved Johnny. Let him see what a good brother and friend he was to Johnny. And fill him with the knowledge of your deep love."

Children grieve. They grieve differently from adults. Their grief is more episodic because the rest of their young life is more episodic. They move from thing to thing—intensely present to the sandbox or easel or football one moment and forgetting about it the next. They can go from deeply missing their brother to admiring a new toy or wanting to go out for ice cream in the space of a half hour—a time sequence that is unfathomable to an adult. They can cry and then go out and play with their friends. But they grieve. Their young hearts are broken. They express their sorrow in different ways.

Thérèse is very different from Gregory. She is the incarnation of all that is social and interpersonal, dramatic and tender. Emotionally, she is more complex. Her personality is a palate of rich and vibrant hues. She wept profusely at the hospital, saying over and over again, "Johnny, please don't die." She was deeply upset because her brother had been hurt.

As with traumatic episodes in my past, some of which took me years to be able to speak about, I knew she could not yet speak about everything she had seen or about what it felt like inside her. Thérèse was processing Johnny's death in fits and starts. On the surface, she wanted to put things back where they used to fit, but the pieces had disappeared. She was trying to push away the memories and the pain because she wanted life to get back to normal, but there were significant blips on the screen. Thérèse needed to make things better for everyone. But she could not make things better for herself. I knew she had a thousand images carved indelibly into her mind. I knew she was hurting. Her pain came out in a thousand different ways. She was constantly telling Maureen and me that she loved us, constantly asking us where we were going and what time we would be home. She craved the warmth and affection of her mother and father and needed the constant reassurance of our love. She did not talk about Johnny's death other than in short, clipped phrases, which, of course, was the clearest sign that she needed to talk more. But I knew I could not push her. She was a mystery to be discovered, not a problem to be solved. Time and love—it would all come out, given time and love. "Keep on talking," I would tell her. Tell the things inside you to someone you trust. I hope it will be God, Maureen, me.

David was hit at the same time as John-Paul. As best we can surmise, John-Paul bore the primary impact and David, the secondary. David is lively, affectionate, and sensitive. He has a face that belongs to a Renaissance angel—something Raphael or Botticelli would have painted. Because he is so sensitive, we tried to give him our undivided attention whenever he spoke in the month after the accident, to see how he was dealing with Johnny's death and to help him along in the process.

Shortly after the funeral we were having family prayer. Toward the end I said to each of the children, "Let's all say something about Johnny." When it came to David's turn he said, "I feel a bit guilty because I'm the one who asked Johnny if he'd like to go ride bikes. Was that a sin?" These are the moments for which nothing in life prepares a parent. I said, "No, David, it's not a sin. Let me tell you what I think happened. I think God looked at Johnny and said, 'Oh that Johnny, I love him so much. He has done everything I wanted him to do in his life. There is nothing he has left undone. And now he is with me forever to be a mighty heavenly intercessor for his family and many other people.' But then God looked at you, David, and said, 'But my David. . . . I love him so much, too, and there's so much more I have for him to do. There are so many people I want to show my love to through him, so many people I want to touch through him. I have so many other things that I want to do in him and for him and through him.' What do you think of that?" "Okay." he said.

A child's grief is no less real than an adult's. And while children are generally not as repressed as adults, neither are they accustomed to talking things out in depth. As parents, we give our children child-sized answers to the problems and mysteries of life appropriate to their stages of development. That is right most of the time. But here the issue was much more complex. A few days after the funeral and our conversation, David's first-grade teacher called Maureen and said that David told her he still felt guilty. And my age-appropriate, child-sized response to David did not begin to consider the issues of God's will, human freedom, the brokenness of the world, the reality of apparently senseless tragedy, and a hundred other questions that I had to grapple with. It was not David's time to struggle with these questions. It was mine.

The day David came home from the hospital we moved Gregory in with him so he would not be alone. In light of this, I listened with some surprise as he said one night, "I'm bored sleeping alone." "David," I said, "you haven't slept alone since the day Johnny died." "Yeah," he said, "but I'm bored sleeping alone." Listen up, Dad, I said to myself. "Tell me why you're bored sleeping alone." "Because Johnny and I always talked before we went to bed."

David and Johnny were like twins—fifteen months apart. They did everything together: came home from school, did homework, went outside, played with their "guys." They would set them up as armies and create entire vistas and scenarios. In fact, once David said, "It's not the same playing guys with the other boys. John did it differently. He knew how to make them *do* things."

David was exhausted for days and weeks after his accident. By dinnertime he often had his head on the table and would ask to be excused to lie down on the couch. He complained of pain in his stomach, leg, and groin. One evening when he was lying on the couch I said, "Okay, David, let's get moving here. Pick up your shorts, let's get our jammies on and get to bed." "Can't everybody just give me a break?" he blurted out in anger. "Don't you see how tired I am?" I looked at him, seeing his weariness. "Okay, David, how about this? I'll pick up your shorts. Then why don't you let me carry you upstairs and put your jammies on and put you to bed. Would that be better?" "Yes."

Another time before going to bed David asked if we could take time to talk about John-Paul. I had promised the children that anytime they wanted to talk about Johnny I would stop what I was doing. David wanted to tell me how much he missed him. All I could say was, "Yes, I miss him too." And then we talked about all the fun things we did with him.

I was aware of a strong impulse to focus on all the remarkably kind and wonderful aspects of Johnny's personality. But that would not be the whole picture. Johnny was not a pious, two-dimensional greeting card. He was flesh and blood, rambunctious and spunky: "A fierce little rogue," as Tadg Dwyer, one of our friends in Ireland, used to affectionately call him.

If he did not like part of a meal, he would store it in one of his cheeks and then ask if he could be excused to go to the bathroom. Once he forgot to flush and Maureen found part of his dinner in the toilet bowl. He learned how to leave the skin on the chicken breast and hide his peas under it. He would not eat bananas because he did not like the seeds. This was my fault. I told him once that the seeds grew into trees and that if he ate the banana, a banana tree might start to grow inside him. He would bug Maureen if he wanted something.

A Grief Unveiled

If they were out shopping near lunchtime he would say, "A hamburger and fries sure would seem good about now." When he finally got them and shared a few with his sisters, he would turn to Maureen and say, "Is I being generous?"

When Johnny would get upset, all of him would get upset. He would stick out his bottom lip and it would begin to quiver, and we all knew we were in for a wail. Sometimes it was because he had been corrected. Sometimes it was because he had make a mistake. One day he left the gate to the deck open. Susanna, who was in her walker at the time, made her way over to it and went flying down the stairs. Miraculously, she landed upright, though she could have seriously injured herself. From two different parts of the house Maureen and I heard the fall and came running. "Did you leave the gate open?" I asked. Johnny cried so hard I thought he would never get over it.

He could become very embarrassed. One night while playing with the children, I grabbed him. I had him by the leg of his pajama pants and as he tried to escape, I held on and his pajama pants came down. He was so mortified, red-faced, tearful, and angry that I wondered if he would ever forgive me.

He would get mad at Rose and pronounce her name with two syllables: "Ro-ose." Maybe it was because she was the next in line. In our family, with rare exceptions, the next-in-line seems to get the emotional exhaust of the one that comes just before.

As we remembered him and encouraged the children to say whatever they wanted about Johnny or the accident or how they were doing, we also discovered how important it was not to superimpose theological truths onto hearts that are broken. To do so simply missed the mark—both for the children and for us. The need we had to somehow refer this all to God and make sense of it was amazing. The only problem was it made no sense at all. We knew that Johnny is in heaven, that he is in no pain, that he is happy. We knew that he does not miss us, at least not in the sense of a "lack," though perhaps he misses us in the sense of anticipation of our future reunion and all the joy that awaits us. We knew that he would not want to come back. If God were a magician and made a deal with us to give him back, we would refuse. After all, how can one trade heaven for earth?

The theological truths are just that—truths, given by revelation to the mind of faith. We were grateful for them, tremendously so. The "eschatological" part of the picture was not a problem. It was a point of joy when we reflected upon it calmly. Johnny's story has a happy ending. That fact did very little to mitigate our dread of the chapter we were going through in our own lives. No, the problem was not theological.

It was the kitchen table that hurt. It was the extra space in the house that hurt. It was the empty seat in the car. It was the driveway too wide as three, not four, children walked home after school. I asked David, "What's the hardest time?" He said, "Playtime. The other kids just don't play like Johnny did." People can say all they want about a brother in heaven. But that does not make playtime any better. Once, he prayed, "Dear Jesus, I thank you for John-Paul and I ask you to bless the man who hit him." After family prayer I asked him why he prayed for the driver. He said, "So he won't feel so bad." He continued, "Dad, I miss John-Paul." "How do you miss him?" "I just see his face everywhere. I see him everywhere." I know this feeling: seeing him everywhere and nowhere. Then his eyes welled up, and I knew that this child's heart was broken. Everything in me wished I could take his grief and pour out my own blood to strengthen him. But I could not. I could only trust that the God who loves him would not give him more than he could endure. So I held him and prayed that Christ's love would heal and console him.

This was our work, as father and mother: to help our children grieve and work through their feelings about Johnny's death; to create an environment where the children felt free to talk about anything on their minds, whether happy, sad, angry, humorous. The only way to help our children was by being their model, by letting them see us grieve. Contrary to what many people think, trying to shield children from grief and pain is one of the most destructive things a parent can do. Their grief is real. The choice is to express it or repress it. If they repress it now they will deal with it over and over again in later life. This is a psychological fact of life. A child who sees a parent grieve will know that it is okay to grieve. For the children to see us grieve had this advantage as well: They know how much we love Johnny. And by inference, they know how much we love them. They know we would miss them this much if they were gone.

They also needed to see us survive, because our example would assure them that they would survive. We needed to give them permission to survive and get better and grow through this experience—and thrive once again, however long it might take and however improbable it might feel at the moment. Watching us gave them permission and showed them how. They were watching us even as we watched over them. They were getting cues from us about faith, hope, love, endurance, sorrow, and so many other things besides. Of course we did not want to overwhelm them with our sorrow. But our great concern was their freedom to talk. So we kept talking about Johnny, but not canonizing. We did not want them competing in an impossible race with their brother the saint.

After dinner one evening, I was having coffee with Maureen. David came into the room and asked if he and I could go somewhere private to talk. I assured him it was fine to talk in front of Mom and asked him, "What's on your mind, son?" "Dad, I'm a teeny bit angry with the man in the car." "Why is that?" I asked. "Because he killed John-Paul." Of course his "teeny bit" angry was like being a "teeny bit" pregnant. There is no such thing.

Just when he seemed as though he was getting back to his normal, bright-eyed, fun-loving self, he answered me thus. David was grieving and grieving deeply. It was ironic to me that the survivor of this tragedy is such a sensitive child. This sensitivity is a two-edged sword. It enabled him to feel the highs and lows more keenly. I hoped it would keep him open to the healing touch of God. For the moment, though, this seven-year-old boy climbed into my arms and started to weep. It was infuriating to be so unable to take his pain. Fathers protect their children, and I could not protect him from this pain. I could only guide him through it.

"David, the truth is that Johnny was killed in a car accident. The driver didn't want to hurt Johnny or you. That is important to understand—he had no desire to hurt you or John-Paul. I'm sure he has wished a thousand times that he could re-do those few seconds of his life. Now, let's talk about the anger. First of all, I understand your anger. It's okay to be angry. Anger is a feeling, and there's nothing wrong with feelings. It's what you do with those feelings that can help you or harm you. You're angry that your best friend got killed. I'm angry, too. It's important to simply admit that to yourself. However, you don't want to live in that anger. How do you get free of anger?" "By forgiving the person," he answered. "Right," I said. "You can talk about your anger any time you want with Mom or me.

But you also need to forgive the man who hit you and Johnny. Then your heart will become free. Otherwise, your anger will become a cage that you are stuck in. And we need to pray for him, that he will experience God's love."

Rose was four when Johnny died. A lot went over her head. This was clear at the hospital when she had no conception that the brother she was touching and talking to was brain dead. It was even clearer in the kitchen the morning after the funeral when she asked, "Where's Johnny?" But whatever went over her head went into her heart, as we would later discover.

Susanna was two, blessed with happy memories and a mind too young for sibling grief. Nicole, I imagine, will remember nothing. I think they will each create him in their minds and hearts from the stories we tell them and the pictures they see. I am sure, however, that as they grow they will have moments, poignant ones, and, I hope, gentle ones, of loving a brother they will not know until they are together in heaven.

We buried a child in the Easter season, the season of resurrection. When our couples group went out for an Easter celebration a few weeks after Easter, I said to Maureen, "I don't want to be here. I don't want to talk about the Resurrection while my son is lying in a grave." But I knew we should be there, and I knew we should talk about the resurrection of the dead. For isn't that what hope is all about? What is there to hope for, if not that love will be reunited with love?

Hope tells me with certainty that we will be reunited. Hope tells me with certainty that I shall see him again. Hope is symbolized in Christian iconography by an anchor. And what does an anchor do? It keeps the ship on course when wind and waves rage against it. But the anchor of hope is sunk in heaven, not on earth. Is this why the saints seem so eccentric to us? Their anchor is sunk in heaven, and their force of gravity is upside down. Their gait, while completely natural to them, looks like dancing on the ceiling to us.

In this early season of grief I was dancing neither on the ceiling nor the floor. I was drunk. I felt the world buzzing around me, as I was trying to maintain my balance while everything looked tilted at a 45-degree angle. On my knees was the only position where everything righted itself. On my knees was the only place where I could think clearly. On my knees was the place where my heart stopped aching for a moment and my vision returned.

There was one great blessing of the first month: I picked up some film at the photo lab, pictures from the last few months. As I held the envelopes in my hands I prayed that there would be one shot of Johnny and Nicole, a treasure for her to keep. As I shuffled the photographs I saw it: two faces—Johnny's and Nicole's—at her baptism, at the moment the water of life was being poured over her. Her face was looking up, his face looking down, so boyish, so charming, so gleeful—and so full of love.

SEVEN

First Summer

Summer vacation arrived six weeks after Johnny died. We made a decision to return to Long Beach Island on the Jersey shore for two weeks. Maureen had grown up going to Long Beach Island, and I had gone there regularly since high school. For the previous several summers we had gone as a family to the Island. We would go early to escape the crowds. We would swim, play in the sand, eat elephant ears, read books, take walks along the beach, rent videos, go to the water slide once as our big treat, and relish every minute of life with no schedule and no phone. Mass, prayer, and naps were the only givens.

Now we were returning to Long Beach Island once again. We stopped for pizza on the way. As we crowded into the booth, reality intercepted the hustle and bustle of getting ready. I thought to myself, "We're going on our summer vacation and Johnny isn't here." Although neither of us was particularly enthusiastic about a vacation, Maureen and I had decided to keep our plans for one simple reason: to get away from everything and be alone together with the children. Later I would realize something I did not know at the time: we were reeling from the blow. It took six or eight weeks just to begin to realize how much pain we were in. Prior to that, shock, adrenaline, and sympathy had kept us going.

We arrived at the house and unpacked, placing all our gear in its familiar places. Naturally, the first thing the children wanted to do was go to the beach. While Maureen took care of Nicole, I took the other five for a walk. The big ones were having a great time running along the shore while I carried Susanna in a backpack. At one point I looked up and saw them down the beach: Gregory, Thérèse, David, and Rose. I shouted to the sky, the wind, the waves, the Lord: "Yes, but one of them is missing. Don't you see? There should be six, and there are only five. One of them is missing." The feeling of abandonment that accompanies these moments is indescribable, so much so that I've stopped expecting anyone to understand it.

The following day I took a long walk with J.J., who, with Nancy, had rented a house a few miles from us. We had planned earlier in the year to be at the beach together. He asked how we were doing. I said, "It's hard." He said, "I imagine everything's hard right now." "Well, almost," I replied. Staring out to the ocean, I told him, "Everywhere I go I see him, but he's not there. The other night I took the kids for a walk. Everything is like it always was but nothing is the same. I am like a madman in prayer crying out to the Lord of the universe: 'We are in trouble. There's a part of our hearts that's been ripped out of us. You must know what this feels like because you are God and you know everything. You have clearly allowed this to happen because you are all-powerful and you could have prevented it. You are the God of love, and so even your allowing this to happen is within the parameters of your divine love. And the most baffling part of all is that you love us and you love Johnny and you want more of your love revealed in the world through this.'" The rantings of a lover? I hope so.

There were moments that felt normal: playing with the children, watching the sun set on the bay and the moon rise over the ocean, making love with Maureen. They were better than normal—they were occasions of grace. The grief was not unremitting, and there were six other children to care for. We owed them our presence, and we owed each other our presence, as our debt as parents and spouses. Giving our presence helped take our mind off the pain. But these moments were the trim and not the color on the wall. The color on the wall was grief, which ranged from a dull ache to a searing anguish. No matter how deeply Maureen and I love each other, and no matter how much we love the children, there was a stunning, stinging, piercing loneliness at these moments. And the presence of others, no matter how close, did nothing to lessen it.

We were also exhausted—physically, mentally, emotionally. Nicole was almost three months old, and Maureen was nursing her. She was still up at night, and the others were up early in the morning. I was beginning to notice that Maureen could not bear to even begin to feel everything inside her, as though if she let it out it would never stop coming. She fell on the bed each night looking as if she could sleep for years.

Father's Day arrived during vacation. Although one could argue that the holiday was an invention of the retail industry, the day itself underscores a very profound and simple point: Fathers are important. I love being a father. Fatherhood is something in the spirit and blood, something alive in me where the deepest, freshest things are. It is a high tower, a vantage point from which I survey everything else. It is a conductor through which external physical evidence passes into my mind. I filter life through its lens. This does not mean being a father is more important than being a husband or an adopted son of God. These three aspects of my life are a trinity in themselves, infusing and interpenetrating each other in such a way that they are indivisible. I never think of being a father without thinking of Maureen and never think of being a husband without thinking of being a son of God through baptism. These facets of my life are like colors of a rainbow: They cannot be isolated and studied independently.

I look at these children "sprung from my loins," as the Scriptures say, and I feel something that goes back beyond ships and commerce and trade, back beyond pharaohs and pyramids and temples, back beyond jungles and huts made of leaf and stalk. What I feel is power. From me came this life dancing before my eyes. But not just from me. From a rich, ripe, sexual union came this life, a union where sensuality redeemed can have its uninhibited sway because it is protected by sacrament and vow. As Ignatius of Antioch said, "The glory of God is man fully alive." These little ones, this life dancing before me, call forth a passion for justice and a desire to protect that draws me beyond myself. This is the kind of feeling that causes fathers to perform heroic feats. It is far different from the wan, limp thing produced by the sexual revolution, much more than simply being the male species that impregnates the female.

Being a father is taking pride in what God has ordained. It is humility and awe before this person who came from me and now stands apart from me. But more than anything, it is gratitude. That I should be the object of such grace is a divine mystery no amount of time or eternity will ever exhaust. No wonder the psalmist says, "What shall I render to the LORD for all his bounty to me?" (Psalm 116:12 RSV).

After dinner on Father's Day, the children lingered at the table and began to talk. They were young, so they affectionately rolled off the litany of thank-yous, for "loving me, playing with

me, tickling me, helping me with my homework." The older
ones added "for correcting me and teaching me." They were
done quickly, and soon everyone was looking at Maureen. They
knew she would know what to say. I looked up and found those
beautiful blue eyes looking into mine. "I want to honor you for
being the father of a saint," she began. "You taught Johnny to
love God. You taught him to love others. You taught him everything he needed to know to get to heaven. You loved him and
delighted in him, and he knew God's love and delight through
you. You were a good father to him, and you're a good father to
all your other children."

We sat there and looked at each other, tears streaming down
our faces, feeling so much love and so much pain in the same
moment. Alone, in the midst of the children, until a little voice
piped up, "Can we go for a walk along the beach tonight? I
promise we won't get our clothes wet."

On the Fourth of July we took the children to the parade. At
one point the sirens from the fire engines began to shriek. The
moment was an invasion for Maureen: The sound brought
back the whole picture of chaos and terror, police cars, ambulances, people running and screaming. When we got home she
told me how hard it was for her. "There's something in me that
just doesn't want to go back there," she said, referring to the
events of April 24 and the week that followed. "I know I have
to, but when it comes near I keep putting it out of my mind
because I don't think I can handle it yet."

Mid-July brought David's birthday. Maureen threw a party
for David and his friends. She kept imagining Johnny there.
"Wouldn't he have loved the party—the gifts, the swimming,
the treats?" We both knew we can't compare heaven's joys to
the tidbits we taste on earth. But neither is it possible to describe
how difficult it is to move through these moments without him.

I am tempted to say that the first summer was a disaster. But that would be untrue. We helped each other through the first summer. Maureen and I grew more deeply in love with each other the first summer because we brought more ingredients to our relationship: sorrow, brokenness, pain. We brought a hope in Christ's victory over death that burned brighter than ever, a deeper gratitude for all our children and a desire never to take them for granted, and a particular prayer of thanks, as we looked at David, that we were spared burying two children. And we brought to our relationship the faith to trust that God was walking us through this season. God was as close as the air we breathed, loving us until our grief exhausted itself on the shores of his heart.

EIGHT

I Will Speak to You in Dreams

"I've been dreaming about Johnny lately," Maureen told me. He had been appearing to her in dreams. The dreams began about six weeks after Johnny died and continued regularly for several months. On an emotional level, six weeks is desolate beyond anyone's ability to touch. She felt an anguishing loneliness for him, a mental pain so intense that it was frightening at times. And in these moments, Johnny began to appear.

"Last night," she began, "I dreamt we were at the beach with the children and I saw this little blond boy with a yellow and blue bathing suit just like Johnny's. I said, 'It's John-Paul!' and I ran over to him. Just as I was about to hug him I realized it wasn't him at all." Maureen started crying. I started crying. And there we were—alone together, barely able even to touch each other's sorrow except for the knowledge that we shared it together.

Once she began talking, the dreams poured out. "Another time Johnny came into our bedroom like he did every morning and climbed on top of you. He was just there, lying on top of you. Gazing at me and smiling. I just looked at him. I wanted so much to touch him, but I knew if I touched him he would disappear. So all I could do was look. But I felt so happy just looking at him.

"Not too long after his death I had a dream from when we lived in Ireland. In my dream, Johnny was a young boy, and

74

he sat atop a stone wall. He was dressed as if to go to church. He was absolutely aware of all that was going on below him. It was clear that he was 'other than' the rest of us. Below the wall were several women. I was one of them, and my friend Carmel Daly from Cobh, who was Johnny's special 'buddy,' was also there. There was no conversation or activity other than the knowledge that John was there and that he was laughing at us and with us. I awoke, realized I had dreamt of him, and immediately experienced a clear awareness of his happiness and a profound comfort at the sense of having been with him."

Maureen continued, "Another morning I awoke and realized that I had had another dream of Johnny. In this one he was about four years old. He was wearing a pair of madras shorts. He flew into the kitchen and grabbed me around my legs. I was standing in front of the 'fridge. I again felt great satisfaction and comfort at having been visited by my son.

"In one dream we were praying with the community. John-Paul was dressed in his Sunday clothes: white oxford shirt, plaid pants, blue belt. In the dream, I knew that Johnny was going to be hit by a car. I was aware that he was gone and yet mysteriously present at the gathering. At the same time he did not know that he was going to die. I was in great anguish thinking that I was going to have to let him go again and that I was going to have to tell him that he was going to suffer and die. 'How will I tell him? How will I tell him?' This question repeated itself over and over in my mind. I awoke, not comforted, but remembering, remembering it all again.

"Some weeks later, my dream was set in some kind of medical setting. It was not quite a hospital but some antiseptic-smelling place. John-Paul was hurt—his leg in particular was very badly hurt." I could see in her eyes that she was recalling that Johnny's leg had in fact been broken in the accident and we had watched the doctor wire his leg while he was on the respirator. Quietly, she went on, "My heart was so frightened, so anguished that he was hurt and in pain. I wanted to take it all away, to make it all better. I picked up Johnny and carried him down a hall to his bed. I awoke with an overwhelming feeling of having carried him, hugged him, touched him. These are all the things I longed to do. I was comforted for a while after this dream.

"In yet another dream, our family was gathered together in the living room. John-Paul was there, bent over, arms crossed, laughing heartily, red-faced. He was trying to engage David in his joke or scheme. He wanted 'Dave' to enjoy this hysteria with him. He was happy and very well.

"Once in my dream a group of women were in a cathedral. Nora, Johnny's kindergarten teacher, spoke up. 'To show you that Johnny's in heaven, we're going to ask him to make crowns appear on the statues of Mary and Joseph and St. Patrick.' All of a sudden, a crown of twinkling lights appeared on Mary's head. More remarkable, though, was that we could see Johnny sitting above the whole scene, dressed in his long blue pants and his white shirt, legs pulled up and arms wrapped around them. He was surveying this whole scene with an expression that was somewhat bemused—a kind of 'So what? big deal!' Then he saw me. He got so excited that he started shouting, 'Mom, Mom, Mom, Mom,' like he always did at home—and he flew down and started hugging me and kissing me. It was so real I could almost feel him. And then I woke up."

A mother's dreams. The Bible has strong words about dreams: strong words in favor, strong words against. Before the prophets came into prominence in Israel, dreams were one of God's main channels of communication. In several passages, God himself appears in the dream: "But God came to

Abimelech in a dream one night . . ." (Genesis 20:3). "Jacob
. . . had a dream. . . . And there was the LORD standing beside
him . . ." (Genesis 28:10–13). "But that night God appeared
to Laban the Aramean in a dream and warned him" (Genesis
31:24). "In Gibeon the LORD appeared to Solomon in a dream
at night" (1 Kings 3:5). At other times, an angel of the Lord
appears in the dream. In the New Testament, the accounts surrounding the birth of the Lord are full of dreams.

Dreams are also relegated to the realm of the ephemeral and
illusory: "Like a dream he takes flight and is not found again; /
he fades away like a vision of the night" (Job 20:8). "As when a
hungry man dreams he is eating / and awakens with an empty
stomach, / Or when a thirsty man dreams he is drinking /
and awakens faint and dry . . ." (Isaiah 29:8). According to
Scripture, dreams can be a revelation of God himself, a means
by which his messengers communicate to us, or an unreal
phantom. The book of Sirach warns that fools are borne aloft
by dreams and likens the one who believes in them to a man
who catches at shadows or chases the wind. Dreams are unreal,
Sirach says, and cautions that what one already expects, the
mind depicts. There is, however, a caveat to his protestations:
The dream is useless unless it be a vision specially sent by the
Most High. When Scripture gives mixed reviews such as these,
the implication is clear: Proceed with caution.

What can I say about Maureen's dreams? For the most part,
they brought comfort. That is the best thing I can say about
them. In that sense, they were visions sent by the Most High.
The word Maureen spoke most often when relating her dreams
to me was "comfort." They were also cathartic. They brought
Johnny near, and in so doing they brought joy and sorrow
near. They were one means by which Maureen could come to
accept all the pain she had been dealt, rather than fighting it or

running from it. They charmed her by bringing his presence close, and then invited her to remember and surrender.

But they did more. They had an iconic quality: They pointed us in the direction we had to go. They led to moments of clear insight. After the first few dreams of Johnny, Maureen said to me, "I really want to go to heaven to see Johnny, but I'm struck that I want to go almost more to see him than to see Jesus." I knew how she felt. While there was no guilt attached to this feeling (for who better than the Lord knows the depths of a parent's heart?), we both agreed that it was a commentary on our relationship with the Lord and where it needed to grow. If only we could long for heaven and long for Christ as we long for our son. And yet at the same time, Christ in John-Paul—the light, the life, the joy, the laughter, all that attracted us and beckoned us and that we found so irresistible about him—was this not also Christ calling us?

I suspect that our longing for those who precede us into God's presence echoes or models in some way the longing we have to be with God himself. Surely this must be, for all that is beautiful partakes in the beauty of Christ. "For from the greatness and beauty of created things / their original author, by analogy, is seen," Wisdom tells us (Wisdom 13:5). Maureen and I had begun to pray that our longing for John-Paul would be eclipsed by a longing for Christ, in whom all things and all relationships find their true and perfect fulfillment.

I am tremendously grateful that Maureen had these dreams. Between the death of Johnny and the birth of Nicole, the other children's needs and her own exhaustion, she had little time to sit down and process what had happened, much less probe the theological issues. God, meanwhile, brought his healing love to her through these images and experiences.

Except for David, the children had not dreamt about Johnny. David told me the only dream he remembers: "Johnny and I were by a ledge, swimming in the water. While we were swimming, we saw a fin coming towards us. Then Johnny got swept out to sea. When I looked at him he was treading water. Just treading water. I thought the fish was a shark, but then I thought it was a whale."

This was not a comforting dream, either to have or to hear about. The shark is a symbol of evil or danger. Danger comes near and Johnny gets pulled away from his brother. Was he also pulled away from the shark? When I asked David about it, he said the "fish with the fin" did not attack them. He also said Johnny was not drowning, but treading water. Treading water suggests waiting. Johnny was swept away, but he is alive, and he is waiting. I said to David, "I think perhaps Johnny wants you to know he's waiting for you. Not in any scary way, not in the sense that you're going to die soon. But simply this: He's watching out for you and waiting for the day you will be together again."

Comfort, joy, and sorrow (and sometimes terror) come together in dreams. Dreams allow the mind, through images and sometimes through words, to come to grips with paradoxes that the rational mind cannot quite fit together.

My dreams about Johnny began several months after Maureen's. In one, I was standing in the kitchen. It was about 2:30 P.M., the time that the children would normally come home from school. Suddenly, Johnny came tripping up the stairs, all happy and smiles—he even had on the yellow and blue fleece overshirt that he wore all last year. I cried, "Johnny!" and grabbed him and hugged him close to me. I could feel the musculature of that strong little body underneath his clothes. I could feel his sturdy ribs and joints and limbs. I said, "Johnny, this can't be. You're dead." And all he did was look at me with that adorable smile. And then I woke up. But I felt happy.

Why does the mind do these things? No doubt to help us put together the deep, unresolved aspects of our lives. Perhaps the unconscious mind is simply more open than the conscious one is. While I am not about to canonize dreams categorically, I know that I felt as though I had touched him. The dream renewed the hope of resurrection that I carried in my heart.

Months after Johnny died I was in Phoenix at a conference of leaders of various Christian communities in North America. I was meeting people I had not seen since Johnny died. I went through the story again and the condolences again. Once again, the wound opened up afresh and the scab ripped off. Once again I found myself in serious pain. By the time I went to bed I felt as raw and vulnerable as when Johnny had been dead only a few weeks. So heavy. So much heartache. I said to him, "Come on, Johnny, you have to help me. You've got to help me get through this. Say something to me. Communicate something to me."

I finally fell asleep, and then I saw him. In the dream Johnny was standing there, hands hanging from his sides. He said nothing. He did not look happy. He did not look sad, but he did not look happy. He looked sober, serious. I felt as though he were saying to me, "Dad, you need to let go of me, of this, of the pain and the heartache, at a deeper level. You need to let go more." The message was simple. The problem was that I did not want to let go. I wanted to return, to retrieve, to bring life back to where it was. But I could not. So each "crisis" moment was a letting go at a deeper level than before—sometimes to an infinitesimally small degree, barely noticeable even to me, but a shade nonetheless.

One night Maureen and I both dreamt about him. He was wearing his white gym shorts and his long-sleeved, striped T-shirt. He was reaching up for me to grab him and said no words. Maureen commented, "He probably wants to be close to us today."

The shock continued to reverberate in my mind and soul. I would think of him or see his photograph, and I would say, "Did this really happen? Have we really gone through all this?" Or, as David said one night, "I wish it was a bad dream." I was not really asking the questions in the literal sense, as though I thought he might be alive. Rather, I kept on asking the questions because my soul would admit his death only a bit at a time. I had to keep going over it, to keep taking it in at deeper and deeper levels, to keep on accepting that all this really has happened and that our lives are irrevocably changed because of it. Part of accepting it was recognizing that I had no say and no choice in the matter, and dealing with the resultant anger. It was a matter of letting go of an understandable but false sense of control that I had no right to have in the first place.

Maureen had hard times when she was tempted to get angry with God and his plan, tempted to think this was all too difficult. One morning as we talked she told me of another dream. "I said to John-Paul last night, 'Johnny, you've got to help me. You've got to communicate more with me.' And then I had a dream. Johnny was a baby, about ten months old. You know how they are when you get them up from their naps and they're sleepy, and they find that crook in your neck and just nestle in? That's how it was: I was holding John-Paul as a little baby, and he just dug into me and nestled in. It made me so happy—just to know he was there."

These dreams gave comfort, challenge, direction, and hope. In these moments, he was very close. But he was in a different medium. He was so light, so bright; we were so dull and heavy. He was present, though in a very different way—present but not "touchable." The fruit, however, was almost always the same: deeper peace and deeper hope. And, yes, a feeling of having been visited.

NINE

The Scriptures and Grief

Two months ago we buried John-Paul. Without thinking, I measured each day in terms of its proximity to the events: Monday—the accident, Tuesday—the pronouncement of death, Wednesday and Thursday—the wakes, Friday—the funeral. Dates and appointments were fixed in relationship to the moment Johnny died.

Cecilia David, the organ transplant coordinator, called one day to ask how we were. "It's very difficult," I said, "but we're trying to live one day at a time. Our faith gives us the sure hope of seeing him again, but the hope does not replace the pain."

I had the distinct impression from those whose training lies in medicine or psychology that we must not try to move too quickly past our grief. Evidently many people do this. Consciously or not, whether responding to an inner fear or the expectations of what recovery looks like to the society around them, many bereaved individuals try to get "back to normal" in a way that ultimately contributes to later, deeper illnesses, whether physical or mental. To me, the thought of moving too quickly past my grief was as absurd as it was impossible. Grief is the price I must pay for love. C.S. Lewis says it well in *The Four Loves:*

Even if it were granted that insurances against heartbreak were our highest wisdom, does God himself offer them? Apparently not. Christ comes at last to say, "Why hast thou forsaken me?" . . . There is no safe investment. To love at all is to be vulnerable. Love anything, and your heart will certainly be wrung and possibly broken. If you want to make sure of keeping it intact, you must give your heart to no one, not even to an animal. Wrap it carefully round with hobbies and little luxuries; avoid entanglements; lock it up safe in the casket or coffin of your selfishness. But in that casket—safe, dark, motionless, airless—it will change. It will not be broken; it will become unbreakable, impenetrable, irredeemable. The alternative to tragedy, or at least to the risk of tragedy, is damnation. The only place outside Heaven where you can be perfectly safe from all the dangers and perturbations of love is Hell.

To love is to risk heartbreak. The depth of grief is proportionate to the depth of love, and it is different for each relationship. How could I compare my grief over Johnny's death to another father's? Maureen's grief to another mother's? The children's to that of other children? Grief is as unique as the individual grieving. Apart from the act of dying itself, I think it is the most solitary journey one ever makes. My grief had not yet found a bottom on which to stand. There was, as of yet, no point from which to begin my climb upward. It is true that faith is a sure anchor. For the moment, however, the chain was still letting out. I had to consent to let the time be what it was.

I realized at the same time that I also had to go outside myself for wisdom. Otherwise I would run the risk of my world imploding. I searched the Scriptures for wisdom on how to grieve. I looked for Biblical characters who were grieving losses. I read each of the more than two hundred passages that mention the words "grief" and "mourning." And what did I find? No neat formula. Rather, I found ringing affirmations of what I instinctively knew to be true: a story in both the Old and New Testaments the glorious ending of which kept inserting itself into the present dark chapters of my life as if to say that no chapter is the whole story, and the middle has no meaning without the beginning and the end. I found a story of ultimate joy.

The Book of Job was a light in the darkness. Why? It gave me two life-changing realizations. First, the Creator does not have to give answers to his creatures. God never tells Job why all his troubles have befallen him. He never tells him it is all a test to see if he loves him beyond his own self-interest. Second, God reveals himself to Job. At the right moment, after all the struggle (not before it), the sublime reality becomes clear. Job hears the voice of God. In that awesome, mysterious, majestic presence, Job's questions are not answered. They simply vanish. When Job finally speaks, he utters words that are at the heart of the Biblical revelation. "I had heard of thee by the hearing of the ear, but now my eye sees thee; therefore I despise myself, and repent in dust and ashes" (Job 42:5–6 RSV). Job helped me see (once again) that I did not need to understand God for the relationship to continue, that the end of understanding is not the end of love, trust, and obedience, but perhaps it is only the beginning.

Another father whom I grew to love was David, the father of Absalom. Upon hearing the news that his son had been killed, he uttered some of the most poignant lines in the Old Testament. "He said as he wept, 'My son Absalom! My son, my son Absalom! If only I had died instead of you, Absalom, my son, my son!'" (2 Samuel 19:1). Here is all the pathos of a father's heart, the endless repetition of a name, and a relationship now gone. Here is the deepest father-wish known: to have given his life for the son to whom he gave life. Job and David taught me that I could miss Johnny this ferociously, grieve him this deeply, and not be losing my mind. These witnesses held out a hand to me in the dark.

Of all the voices, however, the one that spoke the loudest and most clearly was the voice that said nothing. "Standing by the cross of Jesus were his mother, and his mother's sister, Mary the wife of Clopas, and Mary Magdalene" (John 19:25 RSV). Another time, another mother, this one watching her son die. But this mother watches innocence itself die. This mother watches God die! What must it have been like for Mary to suffer the passion and death of her son?

As I sat in my chair meditating on this passage, I looked up. Eye-level with me was the Vladimir icon of the Madonna and Child. Mary was gazing, motionless, with that expression of tenderness and pity that is unique to a mother. It was a look as if to say, "I understand. I too lost a son." She was not trying to cure the pain or make the pain go away. She was simply present. For a moment I was tempted to say, "But you lost him for only three days, and then you got him back. I probably have 40 years without him." I caught myself, realizing what a useless train of thought this would be. After all, with a heart unsullied by sin and therefore infinitely more sensitive to pain and suffering than mine, who is to say that her grief at the foot of the cross was not far greater in an instant than mine would be in a lifetime?

It is hard to imagine how Mary must have experienced the passion of her Son. It is hard because I am the one who is in sin, whose mind is darkened: I cannot imagine correctly or vividly enough. I am the one who caused her Son's passion and her pain. No, I cannot imagine. Even if Mary waited in hope for the promises of God to be fulfilled, what could compare with her grief at living the Passion alongside her Son? Who suffered more—the Son, or the Mother watching her Son, helpless to help him? This had been Maureen's greatest pain: not being able to hold Johnny as he lay in the hospital, not being able to help him. She told me that when she arrived at the hospital she wanted to scream at every nurse, doctor, friend, and family member, "Get out of here and leave me alone with my son!" What must it have been like for Mary to live these moments alongside Jesus, knowing who he was? Simeon says to her, ". . . and a sword will pierce your own soul too—so that the secret thoughts of many may be laid bare" (Luke 2:35 NJB). What a mysterious announcement! Understanding the thoughts of others is tied to having one's own heart pierced by a sword. How different are God's ways!

The psalms were my other place of refuge. They describe the emotion of grief in tremendously evocative language. This is all the more striking when one realizes they were written by men, since men, it is widely assumed, do not and should not give in to such strong emotions. But these men, so poetic and prophetic, do just that. They cry out to God, "How long must I carry sorrow in my soul,/grief in my heart day after day?" (Psalm 13:3a). They are unafraid of God. They tell him that their eyes are wasted with grief, and their souls and bodies are spent. They tell him they are bent over in mourning, that they rock with grief, that they groan under the weight of their sorrow. And they are the world's greatest teachers of prayer!

Scripture even goes so far as to link the origin of the cult of idols to a father's mourning over the sudden death of his child. "For a father, afflicted with untimely mourning, / made an image of the child so quickly taken from him, / And now honored as a god what was formerly a dead man / and handed down to his subjects mysteries and sacrifices. / Then, in time, the impious practice gained strength and was observed as law, / and graven things were worshiped by princely decrees" (Wisdom 14:15–16).

Obviously, mourning, like anything else, can be taken too far and virtually take on a life of its own. Poignant as the father's distress is, it corresponds remarkably to what psychiatric literature would refer to as being stuck in morbid grief.

And what of Christ himself? What can we say about Jesus weeping at the tomb of his friend Lazarus? I picture his head leaning against the stone, his eyes, his tears, his face, the incline of his body. Is this just a moment in time or did heaven and earth hold their breath? Might we not better imagine that the cosmos keeled and swayed at the pain of its Lord? And if Christ wept thus for Lazarus, what must the Father have done at the broken body of his Son? There is no grief like the grief of God.

We too weep. For us the grief seems endless, the sheer weight of sorrow, crushing. And yet that is not the full picture. Grief and mourning are not the end. Life is the end. Joy and gladness and redemption are the end. As deep as the feelings descend, as poignantly as they are described, they cannot compare with the words God speaks when announcing the season that follows grief—words so light and merry, so full of music that they beg to be sung. God speaks of a better day, a new day coming that has already dawned in Christ, when his chosen ones will enter Zion singing, crowned with everlasting joy. He speaks of the day when sorrow will flee, when virgins shall make merry and dance, when mourning shall be turned into joy.

These words anchored my hope. They resonated far below my emotions. They were a strong, sure light. They were the breath of God in my lungs. They gave my mind moments of freedom and respite in the midst of pain. They were like stars shining in the darkness. They enabled Maureen and me to say to one another, "We will see him again." And they pointed beyond themselves to the end of the story. There, St. John proclaims in words so full of wonder and love, God "will wipe every tear from their eyes, and there shall be no more death or mourning, wailing or pain, [for] the old order has passed away" (Revelation 21:4). These words, which are like Jacob's ladder reaching to the heavens and piercing the veil, reach their climax in the One who overcame death: Jesus Christ, the Son of God.

The full picture is the resurrection. The full picture is Christ before the tomb, banner unfurled, rocks shattered, guards dazed, every muscle taut with the sheer glory of the moment: "I am alive again!" Hope is the final word. The pain is real, at times almost unbearable. But the hope is just as real, and ultimately, more real, for while the pain will disappear and the tears will be wiped away, hope will usher us into the presence of the Lord. Hope tells me with certainty that we will be reunited. Hope tells me with certainty that I shall see him again.

I was beginning to see that it was possible to have joy in the midst of sorrow. I fell in love with the image of Christ being the One who has broken the ancient chains, and I wrote a song, "He Comes Like Morning." I thought of the famous picture that was taken from outer space in which the earth is seen as a small, frail, beautiful globe. In my mind's eye I saw it covered in chains. Ancient chains. Chains as old as the Fall: so dark, so invincible, so heavy. Then I saw these chains burst asunder by the glory of Christ's resurrection. Yet the One who burst them felt all our pain on Calvary. He does not simply dwell with us in our pain, though mercifully, he does do that. Rather, he brings us through pain into newness of life. He has given us a point of reference outside ourselves so we can be saved.

He comes like morning
Clear as air the breath of God
The dawnstar dances to a new song
Trees clap their hands for joy

    He is the One who has broken the ancient chains
    He is the One who has pierced the darkness
    He is the One who has shattered the night
    Into a thousand shining stars

He is my savior
He is the only true light
He shines higher than the heavens
He makes the very darkness bright

    He is the One who has spoken the Father's name
    He is the One who has burst the silence
    He is the One who has felt every pain
    On the hill of Calvary

He comes to set me free
He's like a torrent upon the Earth
Streams of living water
Give every desert new birth

    When I fall down, lose my eyes and my ears
    When I think my heart is being torn in pieces
    I feel a hand with a mark of a nail
    And it's reaching out for me

He is the Lamb He is the Light
He is the One who will lead us safely
Through the gates of the shadow of death
Into a bright new shining day.

TEN

God Has Long Eyes

For three months there was no talk of healing. There was love and tenderness, and a particular concern to make a place for the children where they could speak freely. There were friends who showed their love in countless gestures. And there was freedom, the freedom we gave each other to grieve—to feel the pain of John-Paul's absence in all its harsh and stark reality. But there was no talk of healing.

Toward the end of July the Floyd clan had a family reunion in Vermont. Needless to say, we did not want to join the fun: I was in no mood to celebrate, and Maureen, who was caring for the baby, was not up to it. For my father's sake, I decided to go. I knew Dad would love nothing more than to be surrounded by his sons and their families. Apart from God, there is nothing Dad loves more than family. And while this is true for many men, my four brothers and I have been blessed by a father who told us with words and showed us with deeds that we are his greatest treasure. No small heritage, that. Dad and his sister and three brothers were all well, but they were aging. I realized this might be not just the first, but the last reunion of its kind.

On a bright, cloudless summer morning, I drove up to Sugarbush with Gregory, Thérèse, and David. I figured they could use a change of scenery. I was beginning to notice that I could enjoy life in small pieces. With the children I could careen down an alpine slide, or jump off the rocks into a clear, cool swimming hole, or go out for pizza, or race in the pool. I was delighted to see them laugh, meet lots of cousins for the first time, and pick up where they'd left off with the ones they already knew. I enjoyed their silly jokes. I whispered prayers of gratitude to God that we had been spared burying David. I looked at them for a long while as they slept in the room we shared. Real and true as these highlights were, however, they only punctuated the deeper hues of life without John-Paul. The moments that were really good inevitably brought him back to mind. "Wouldn't he love the chair lift?" the children asked. "Wouldn't he love the alpine slide?" "Wouldn't he love the swimming hole?"

One night after they had gone to bed, I wrote their brother a letter.

Dear Johnny,

You've been dead thirteen weeks. It's beginning to feel like you've been gone for a while. The spaces are growing wider between the moments of intense grief. We are laughing and smiling about other things, even about you. If a guest came to dinner he would think you were across the street at Mike's, so much are you a part of our everyday conversation.

I feel like I'm beginning to breathe again. Yet at the same time, I feel like you're slipping. I read stories of saints who appeared to their parents and I wish you would appear to me and tell me what I already know: "Don't weep for me. Be happy. I'm happy. Dad, I'm so happy!" I don't need you to do this: It would only be to see your face and hear your voice. I already know the message.

It's difficult for people to understand the ambivalence I feel, even about the decrease in my spiritual and emotional pain. Since the pain is so related to my love of you, I do a strange

mathematical equation that pain/grief/suffering equals intensity
of love. Therefore for the pain to lessen feels like distance is
creeping into the relationship. As a consequence, I'm left with
a feeling I wouldn't believe if I didn't possess it: I'm not sure I
want the pain to go away. The pain keeps you close.

In my times of deepest sorrow, my one consolation has been
the knowledge that now you know how much I love you. From
the vantage point of heaven's perfect illumination, I suspect that
everything is much clearer. I will always love you, Johnny. I can't
wait to see you. I am trying to be patient. If I think of not seeing
you for thirty or forty years, the weight of that sorrow crushes
me. But if I ask myself, "Do I have enough grace to go from
breakfast to bedtime without seeing you?" the answer is, "Yes."
I can handle not seeing you today. Not tomorrow. Just today.

Love,
Dad

Things were beginning to level out a bit. I could move
through a day at home or the office giving myself energetically
to Maureen or the children or work. What I could not plan
for were the moments when I would turn a corner and feel as
if someone had slammed a two-by-four against my head. At
such times, I realized I did not have to go looking for grief;
grief would find me.

I was also beginning to understand that I had to give God
permission to heal the pain. Giving God permission means
that if my life is surrendered to Christ, I will not hold onto
anything but him. That even my pain must yield its pride of
place. I realized that in the end, God is the one and only necessity. He is all I need, and when it is my turn to meet him, I
will be alone. At that moment giving God permission meant
that I would yield the seasons of this experience to his care. It

was an act of faith in his tenderness: faith that he would not heal me before I was ready, faith that he would not force me to let go of my attachment to my son in a way I could not yet do. This grace of surrender operates in the mind that says, "I will allow myself to recover," or even just, "I will allow myself this moment of joy." Giving God permission is a paradigm of the absolute necessity of the human intersecting with the divine. Grace always builds upon nature, never replaces it. It was my act of trust that God would not violate the human need to grieve.

There were times when I felt joy and hope when thinking about Johnny. I was not kidding myself; I did not expect grief to be finished. I had noticed that "high-emotion" events triggered these feelings, as did beautiful music, Johnny's favorite songs, or the many small kindnesses that people did. But if "getting over it" is what one does with chicken pox or measles or the flu, there is no "getting over" the death of a child. To get over chicken pox means that it has no meaning and barely any memory in one's life. In this sense we will never get over Johnny's death. That would be absurd.

If that is the case, what kind of healing could I expect? I believe it is this: Ever so slowly, I began to make room for the loss in my heart. This was the healing, or at least its beginning: to make room for the loss in my heart. To learn to live with the loss. The loss did not disappear, but the life around it began to reappear. I embraced the truth, however haltingly, that I have life despite this loss.

As God poured his love into my soul, I began to think a bit more about where Johnny is and a bit less about where he was. More accurately, the colors of where he is became more luminous, and the colors of where he was became more muted. I noticed a rhythm: When the harsh reality of memory or loss came crashing in on the slow softening of my sorrow,

I remembered the wave that spends itself on the shore and recedes—and I knew that the quiet would reappear.

Good moments were followed by difficult ones and vice versa, in seemingly never-ending succession. No sooner did I realize that God was healing me, than I had a moment that made me feel as if I had not even begun to heal. Except for one fact: Such moments were less frequent. This very juxtaposition of joy and sorrow caused me to realize that healing travels at its own appointed pace, led by the Spirit of God, according to what he wanted to teach me and how he wanted to form me. I could only open my heart to God in trust and surrender, realizing that I was not in control. But the fruit of trust is peace.

Letting go is a complex process. The rational mind says, "What do you mean, 'let go'? He couldn't possibly be more gone." Yet the grieving parent holds on to much more than the memory, and indeed we will hold onto that until we see him again. No, I held onto a time line: I related each date to what happened on April 24—one week ago, four weeks ago, three months ago.

I held onto a time line and I held onto pain. "Holding onto pain" sounds crazy unless one has lost someone very dear. But I wrapped the arms of my soul around my pain and guarded it like a treasure. An army arrayed could not have forced open those arms. They would open only when I was ready. God knew this. He was not upset by this, not worried, not offended. He waited. And he beckoned ever so gently. I prayed, "Lord, take away the pain," but I did not really want him to. I said that prayer for the children, I said it for Maureen, but not for myself. I could not pray, "Lord, heal me of Johnny's death," because the prayer made no sense and because I knew intuitively that I had to grieve until I finished grieving. Dietrich Bonhoeffer says it well:

Nothing can make up for the absence of someone we love . . . we must simply hold out and see it through. That sounds very hard at first, but at the same time it is a great consolation, for the gap, as long as it remains unfulfilled, preserves the bonds between us. It is nonsense to say that God fills the gap; God doesn't fill it, but on the contrary, He keeps it empty and so helps us to keep alive our former communion with each other, even at the cost of pain.

Shortly after we arrived home from Vermont our friend Myriam Scanlon came from Ireland to spend the summer with us. Myriam had visited the previous summer as well. We had become friends in 1991 when we lived in Ireland. She was no sooner in the door than the children were telling her stories and plying her with questions. It was not long before the conversation turned to Johnny. I was giving her the conventional scenario about the boys riding their bikes down the driveway and out into the street, about the sunlight, the trees, the bushes, and the driver's inability to see the boys. David interrupted. "That's not what happened at all," he said. "What?" I asked quietly, in front of Maureen, the children, and Myriam. "You know what happened?" "Yes."

"Can you take me outside and show me?" I asked. "Yes," he replied. David walked me down the driveway and past the mailbox. "We were standing right here on the side of the road," he said, gesturing toward the exact location. "We were on our bikes but we weren't riding them. Then, up there," he said, pointing to the Clementes' house, "we saw a car. It kept coming at us. We couldn't move. We were in shock." At that moment I realized something that never made it into the police reports. There was a witness. David. He had seen the car coming. In fact, the last thing he had seen was the car coming at him and Johnny. Thirteen weeks after the accident he told me the details. He told me quietly, peacefully, matter-of-factly. I was stunned. This child saw the car coming at him and his brother.

I wonder how many of these scenarios are packed away inside the minds of the children. How many times will I be surprised by their memories, their pain? How many moments will there be when I am amazed by their resilience? They are marked by this experience, to be sure. But they are marked not only for worse. Their response to Johnny's death also has the potential to change them for the better— if we are faithful, if we handle it right.

Already I could see hints of this change in myself. Until this time I had never really longed for heaven. I believed in it. I made my moral choices in the hope of attaining it. But it was so far beyond my imagination that my attitude had been to embrace God now and trust that I will love him enough to give myself unreservedly to him when the moment comes to exchange time for eternity.

But something had changed. When Johnny's brain stem was snapped, something snapped inside of me—something that tied me to earth, that made the physical beauty and the beauty of the natural world idols to me. Physical beauty rots in the grave and natural beauty groans in travail, while both await their liberation from slavery to corruption. I found myself longing for heaven, longing to be with my son, longing to leave this valley of tears. But more, I was longing to be with God for his own sake. Something in the longing was changing. It was no longer simply to be rid of the pain. It was no longer simply to see Johnny again. It was God himself who was the longing behind all my other longings. God himself was the fulfillment of all that I glimpsed in the nobility of my friends, the sweetness of my family ties, the heroism of those who work for justice. God himself was the beauty I sought in all the beauty that so delighted my soul and senses. It was God who used even pain to call me to himself. Even pain? No, that is not correct. Rather, as C.S. Lewis says in *The Problem of Pain*, "God whispers to us in our pleasures . . . but shouts in our pains: It is His megaphone to rouse a deaf world." And when things were at their worst, I kept going back to the Book of Revelation: "There will be new heavens and a new earth. . . . He will wipe every tear from their eyes, and there shall be no more death or mourning, wailing or pain, [for] the old order has passed away" (Revelation 21:4). I returned to this word again and again, drinking in its consolation, because when I absorbed it into the depths of my soul I found peace.

There will be a time when every tear is wiped away. There will be a time when sorrow and mourning and wailing and pain and death will disappear. There will be a time when we are reunited with those we love—if we will but believe, hope, trust, and obey.

After confession one day I was praying before the Blessed Sacrament with my head in my hands. Almost imperceptibly I felt an arm settle on mine and a head look for a place to nestle. It was David. "Are you okay, Dad? Do you miss John-Paul? I bet you miss him more than we do." The suffering of love. The amazing thing about this suffering is that God is present in it in a way that he is not in moments of joy. Certain moments of joy or felicity can almost do without him—there is so much natural goodness to them. But in such sorrow, all is stripped bare. God was a spare but overwhelming presence. I can only conclude that Johnny must have been praying for us.

Could he be? Is this possible? I am aware that within different Christian traditions this is the kind of issue that makes people draw swords. However, as the father of a child who loves me and lives in the presence of the Lord, I have to know whether I am standing on solid ground or wading in the treacherous tides of wish fulfillment. What do the Scriptures say about those who have preceded us into the presence of the Lord? Can I accurately speak of praying to Johnny or of Johnny praying for us?

The Scriptures are abundantly clear that there are two principal intercessors. "In the same way, the Spirit too comes to the aid of our weakness; for we do not know how to pray as we ought, but the Spirit itself intercedes with inexpressible groanings. And the one who searches hearts knows what is the intention of the Spirit, because it intercedes for the holy ones according to God's will" (Romans 8:26–27).

Speaking of Christ, the author of Hebrews says, "Therefore, he is always able to save those who approach God through him, since he lives forever to make intercession for them" (Hebrews 7:25).

The Holy Spirit intercedes for us. Christ intercedes for us. One could say we have no need to ask anyone else to pray for us.

That being the case, why is it that whenever we have a need we turn to a friend and ask, "Would you pray for me?" Why is the request for prayer so immediate, so effortless when it concerns a job change, a loved one, a sick relative, a child who is not doing well? This request for human solidarity in prayer is universal. Surely Christ suffices. We can go to him directly. Why bother with anyone else? And yet does not Christ himself say, " . . . if two of you agree on earth about anything for which they are to pray, it shall be granted to them by my heavenly Father" (Matthew 18:19)? He obviously understands our need for community better than we do.

I believe that as we make our way home to heaven, we pilgrims on earth share a union in Christ with those who are asleep in the Lord. I believe Johnny prays alongside us and asks the Lord to continue to watch over us. My prayer to Johnny is a simple, humble request that he ask the Lord to help us. However I phrase it, my communion with John-Paul is one of brothers sharing a common goal and destiny, though he has arrived and I am still en route.

From another vantage point, why would we think that our friends in heaven are by that fact *less* capable of praying for us than those who are still on this side of the veil? When I pray to Johnny I am not talking about communicating with the dead, or avoiding God or negating the work of Christ. John-Paul does not stand between me and Christ the way Jesus stands between me and the Father. He stands with me as a partner in prayer. I think that the veil between God's saints in this realm and God's saints in the heavenly realm is not as inflexible or opaque as we might believe. Is this not what the author of Hebrews is implying: "Therefore, since we are surrounded by so great a cloud of witnesses, let us rid ourselves of every burden and sin that clings to us and persevere in running the race that lies before us while keeping our eyes fixed on Jesus, the leader and perfecter of faith" (Hebrews 12:1–2)? The cloud of witnesses—is it not the entire company of those who love the Lord and live in his presence? Is this not what St. Paul is hinting at when he writes, "For God did not destine us for wrath, but to gain salvation through our Lord Jesus Christ, who died for us, so that whether we are awake or asleep we may live together with him" (1 Thessalonians 5:9–10)?

We are a family. We are to live together with him whether we are awake or asleep. I have struggled with Jesus and St. Paul referring to the dead as merely asleep. I want to say, "No, Lord, my other kids wake up each morning. Johnny doesn't." But in light of the resurrection of the dead, it is true. We are all going to rise. Wisdom is knowing how brief and how critical this life is in light of eternity.

St. Paul says we live together with Christ whether we are awake or asleep. I live together with Christ, and Johnny lives together with Christ. The deeper I am in union with Christ the more our respective "togethernesses" converge. The closer I am to Christ, the closer I am to Johnny.

As I pondered these mysteries I realized that in my life there were only two principal players in this drama. The driver of the car was almost incidental. I rarely thought of him in terms of the death of John-Paul. I thought of him often in terms of the burden he was carrying. But in reality, this one was between me and God.

This experience changed my relationship with God. In some ways, the relationship felt less intimate. God had become much more "wholly other than," more transcendent. He is much different from what I thought him to be. He is not a father like I am a father. He infinitely transcends the scope of my fatherhood, which would never have allowed this to happen were it in my power to prevent it. But he did allow it. He obviously thinks about family life differently than I do. And while God is more distant mentally and emotionally, he is as present and invisible as the air I breathe. Why? I think it is because I have stopped creating God. From time immemorial men and women have created God in their own image. For many of us, however unconsciously, God is a much bigger and better version of ourselves. I'm good; he is really good. I love; he really loves. I can do things; he can really do things. God even gives us the very anthropomorphic images by which we relate to him: father, shepherd, warrior, king, and a host of others. He both indwells and transcends these images.

I could say God came "more alive" through parts of his Word with which I had hitherto spent little time, but in reality, I was the one who was becoming more alive. He sees the whole picture; I see bits and pieces, shadows, shafts of light. Objectively, I can say "we have a son in heaven." This fact is a point of joy when I reflect upon it calmly. John-Paul is safely home, having accomplished everything in his life that God wanted of him. God has long eyes, eyes that span the course of history. "For a thousand years in your sight are like yesterday, when it is past, or like a watch in the night" (Psalm 90:4 NRSV). God sees the perfect plan he had in mind for John-Paul and its consequences being played out in our lives. Who but God knows how much we need Johnny face-to-face with him on our behalf? Who but God knows what will transpire in our lives and the lives of those who were touched by his life and death? God's long eyes see Johnny's brief and splendid time with us as one movement: life, death, and resurrection. He alone knows the grace that sorrow is working in our souls, the healing that is taking place beneath what we can feel, the joy that is yet to come. To him it is all of a piece.

My relationship with God had changed. And yet, I kept having a recurring image. It was of a pietà. But instead of Mary holding Jesus, it was God the Father, holding the dead body of his Son. It was extraordinarily comforting to me. In the first week of Johnny's death I could only turn to Mary, other than uttering an inchoate "Oh God, help us." Now my spirit was turning to the Father. He experienced the death of his Son infinitely: infinite pain and sorrow in the heart of God. This was incredibly important to me: that God suffers and that he is not immune to, or unmoved by, my suffering.

So I saw the Father, looking down at the body of his Son, and I was one with him in sorrow, one with him in grief. But I was one with him. And here I would stay, leaning all my weight on him.

ELEVEN

The Awful Question

He had approached me back at the house, after the funeral. Most of our family and friends had gone home. "In a few months, when things settle down a bit, you and Maureen are going to need a break. I'm sending you to Bermuda for a week." It was the sort of command only a close friend could give. "There are two conditions," he continued. "First, nobody knows about this except you, Maureen, and me. Second, you have to take Maureen to dinner at the Four Ways and charge it to my account." The Four Ways, we would later discover, is one of the most elegant restaurants in Bermuda.

August arrived. We drove the three older children to camp, farmed out the three little ones, and flew to Bermuda. Bermuda was sheer gift. The time away together nourished us on many levels. One was the rest. Maureen and I were both amazed at how exhausted we were. It seemed as though there was a subterranean stream of exhaustion that we tapped into whenever the normal "day-to-day" tiredness of work and caring for the children subsided a bit. It was an exhaustion, especially for Maureen, that came from someplace deep within her. To have nothing to do for a week was an enormous gift.

Another level on which we were nourished was the visual. Bermuda is exceptionally beautiful. The sand truly is pink, the water is every color of blue, and the shoreline has lots of rocky outcroppings that look like a kind of freeform sculpture carved by the ocean. We spent hours swimming, walking the beaches, lying quietly next to each other saying nothing, simply relishing the sound of the waves and feeling the warmth of the sun on our bodies. We rented motorbikes and traveled inland and found manicured gardens and pastel-colored buildings, along with a very British feeling both in the order and in the polite reserve of the inhabitants. The juxtaposition of nature's extravagant hand and the "man has taken dominion" sense of cultivated beauty gives Bermuda its particular charm. All this and glorious weather besides. As the psalms so clearly reveal, the beauty of the physical world is a conduit to God. How often they begin at nature and end in God. So it was with us: The time, the space, the expanse, the beauty, lifted our souls and drew us into his presence.

We also allowed ourselves to have fun. Without guilt. Without self-recrimination. Strange as it sounds, we had to give ourselves a kind of subconscious permission to do this, daring to let go of Johnny for a few hours at a time. We had to learn by experience that it did not insult Johnny's memory to have a good laugh or a good time or a good night out. We gave ourselves permission to realize how much we have and not only how much we have lost. I knew this was exactly what Johnny would love to have seen us doing. But we had to yield to it. We went from beach to beach, explored hidden nooks, went into little shops, visited galleries.

And we went to the Four Ways. Maureen was tanned from the sun and looking a lot more rested. I had bought her a royal blue dress the day before. I sat across from her in the idyllic setting of the restaurant with its fountains and courtyards and candlelight and watched the color of the dress play with the blue of her eyes. I thought to myself, "How beautiful you are."

I kept looking at her, relishing the gift that she is, realizing that we were growing more deeply in love with one another. I also realized that I was feeling decidedly romantic!

The best part of the week was the time to talk. We talked a lot about Johnny and the experience of the last four months. We talked about each of the children and how they were doing. We talked about what it means to have a son in heaven. We talked like this because we had the time. We needed time to express to God and to each other all the good and bad things going on inside us: all the crazy, irrational, hopeful, angry, sublime, hurting, and healing pieces that made up the mosaic of the last few months. The fruit of these conversations was ripe indeed: They helped us to figure out what was true and what was false, what to hold onto and what to discard. There were many moments when we would pause in our conversations, and pain would shoot through either one of us like an arrow. Many moments we would turn away and look out the window. And there were plenty of tears. But we experienced lots of laughter, too, and the joy and comfort that our relationship brings.

Somehow this experience forged a deeper bond between us than I ever thought possible. And I mean *forged,* as in, hammered into a new shape in the furnace of extreme pain. We came to know one another better than before, to see one another more clearly and rely on each other more deeply. We acquired a new knowledge, one that told us not much could be worse than this but that this would not kill us. It was making us stronger. I remember a conversation from this time. It was one of those rare, private, quiet moments. We were lying in bed. I looked over at her, eyes closed, body spent, savoring the silence and the peace.

I asked her, "How are you?"

"I miss him a lot," she replied. "I've been so exhausted and so busy I don't have much time to think, but when I do, I miss him a lot."

"Why do you think God took him home?"

"Because he loves him and he loves us."

What does one make of such a conversation? It is rife with challenges: the language, the theological presuppositions, the weariness, the pain. But Maureen's answer stunned me. "Because God loves him and he loves us." It was at once mystical and absurd, simple and complicated, paradoxical and utterly mysterious. It came from a mother of an infant who had told me she had no time to grieve. A mother who kept finding her dead son's things everywhere she turned. A mother who still made one sandwich too many in the morning, who waited for him to come tripping up the driveway after school. A mother with six other children who have constant needs of a "mothers only" sort, combined with their own grief and bewilderment. A mother who, looking at her son who survived, had come to recognize a look on his face that she could only describe as lost. A wife with a husband whose seasons of grief were utterly different from her own.

I tried to comfort her. I told her she was grieving by inches, not by miles, because that was all she had room for at the moment. I told her the time would come when she would be able to fully feel what had happened and work it through. That time was not now, I told her. She was exhausted, and there were too many other needs demanding her attention. She was the only one who could be mother to all these children. I suspected that she was grieving not only the loss of her child but the fact that she did not have the luxury of grieving her son properly.

And yet she answered my question "Why did God take him home?" with the confident words "Because he loves him and he loves us." Was it an unrehearsed flash of intuitive, spiritual brilliance? Was it something she felt she had to say? I did not know. I did know it was her first response, and as such, it was noteworthy.

First responses sometimes perfectly capture and express what we are trying to say. They often embarrass us because they so clearly tell us the condition of our hearts. At other times, we must retrieve them and admit that they did not do justice to our thoughts or feelings. Those thoughts and feelings were either more complex or more simple, darker or lighter, more clouded or clearer than what our words conveyed. In the attempt to give voice to my soul, I was confronted with the problem of language.

The question, the answer, and the language they employ were all problems because two boys on my front lawn, one dead and one wounded, is a problem. It is a problem that no philosophy or theology could solve. Why? Because all the philosophy and theology in the world could not touch my pain. Yet even in my pain I still had to wrestle with the awful question: Why?

Wrestling is a good Biblical sport. Jacob wrestled with the angel at Peniel and would not let go until he received the blessing he sought (Genesis 32). The angel renamed him Israel, because he had contended with divine and human beings and had prevailed. This is a remarkable passage. Jacob receives a blessing because he fought! He obviously was not afraid of God. Job wrestled with his "friends" and with God himself by vehemently protesting his innocence in the face of tragedy. Jesus wrestled with his Father's will in Gethsemane: "Abba, Father, all things are possible to you. Take this cup away from me, but not what I will but what you will" (Mark 14:36). Anguish and sweat pour like blood: there is no facile acceptance here, but profound, unspeakably profound surrender. In these incidents and in many others, the dynamic is wrestle and surrender. The wrestling is between God and humanity, and it is as old as death. But it does not appear to be a sign of rebellion or pride. God created the mind that questions and the heart that feels, and thus the need to understand. It is part of our transcendence, part of being "in his image." And so I had to wrestle with God, if only to come to the point of realizing that there are some things I may never understand.

God is unafraid of the wrestling. He is always waiting, ready to engage. He never told Jacob to stop fighting. He never told Job his protestations were arrogant, though he did call them ignorant at one point (Job 38:2). No matter. Job himself said, "What wonder then if my words are wild?" (Job 6:3 NJB). Such are the extremes of suffering. God never told Jesus his anguish and fear were "out of place" for the Son of God, or that his request to let the cup pass was unworthy of him. Thank God. It is because of these struggles and questions that I can find a home in his word.

Ultimately, the key is acceptance and surrender. But first, I had to wrestle. And what I wrestled with is "What do suffering and evil say about the power and love of God?" The classic arguments are not hard to understand: God is either all-loving and not all-powerful (represented by his inability to stop this tragedy from happening), or God is all-powerful but not all-loving (represented by his unwillingness to stop this tragedy from happening). Either way, suffering and evil are a scandal.

My question "Why did God take him home?" presupposes that God took him home. Did he? Again language falters. Technically, no. There was no theophany, no voice, no chariot and horses. There was no hand reaching down or whirlwind gusting him up. No disappearance like Elijah's, no assumption like Enoch's. These God took. Johnny was not one of them. I am certain God received him with open arms, but I am not at all sure that he took him. "Taking him" by means of a car crash makes God the agent both of his death and of the undoubtedly great suffering of the man who hit him, to say nothing of all the other sufferings involved. The God of life does not go around setting up accidents. They happen because we live in a world broken by sin, a world of human freedom, and a creation that still groans in travail while awaiting its redemption.

And yet, to be more honest than I want to be, I cannot attribute Johnny's death to "just an accident," as though God were nowhere near it. I cannot forget that Johnny talked about heaven more than all the other children. I cannot forget his fascination with it, or his concern about whether he would make it. I cannot forget that shortly before he died he asked Maureen if she thought he would be going to heaven soon. And so I am confronted by the awesome and terrible prospect of a God and a boy who were speaking with one another in a realm of the Spirit of which I cannot conceive. Was God asking of him permission to make of his life a sacrifice, some kind of an offering, some kind of a gift? I do not know. Was God whispering in his soul? I could not deny it if my life depended on it.

At a certain point I must stop asking why. If I keep asking why, and insist on discovering an answer, I will drive myself insane. The finite human mind cannot reach into the recesses of the infinitely transcendent mind of God. God does not choose to reveal to us everything. He does not have to. He is God. And I may not speak to him as though he and I were on equal ground in opposing teams in a debate. He is Creator and I am creature. But the end of understanding does not mean the end of trust or love or obedience.

Sometimes I picture in my mind's eye God showing me when I get to heaven why all this happened. It looks like the diagram of the London Underground: "Well, this happened here because of Johnny's death," and "he talked to her and she got touched," and "these people came to know me. . . ." It is an imaginative excursion at best. Actually, I think that when I get to heaven one of three things will happen. Either God will tell me why he allowed Johnny to die in this tragic accident, or I will be so overjoyed to see Johnny again that I will not care, or I will be so enraptured by God that every question will simply vanish. Whatever the case, I will join him in his eternal Now.

And so I reached the point where I could only surrender to the mystery of God's will in the broadest sense of the word. At a certain point, a moment of grace, God's will ceases to be a problem and becomes a mystery. I admit that I do not know about these things. I know that I will not answer this question and that is my act of faith: to believe with the unanswered question. I must accept that God allows things to happen that he did not design, or accept that his designs, which initially transcend my capacity to understand, rest preeminent and secure and are never ultimately thwarted by evil.

God permitted the accident to happen for reasons only he knows. He loved Johnny's life on earth and he loves his life in heaven. He both grieves for our pain and rejoices that his son is home. How can he do this? How can he be love and be the indirect cause of so much pain? It is beyond human reckoning. But not beyond faith. Because the way to heaven is the way of the cross. Every life has its measure of suffering. God requires suffering, and even became suffering for us to show us that suffering is not just not evil, but is, in fact, part of the road that leads to heaven. God loves suffering not as an end in itself, but for what it can make us and where it can lead us.

Suffering is the heat that softens our hearts. In Jeremiah and Ezekiel, God calls our hearts stony. If the prophets were writing today, perhaps they would call our hearts steely: sleek and shiny, reflecting the world around them; cold and hard. God uses suffering to anneal our hearts so that with the hammer of his grace he may shape them into more perfect, suitable vessels. When the metal is hot, it bends easily, and the slightest touch of the hammer produces the desired effect. To have suffered deeply and accepted that suffering enables us to be one with others in their suffering. St. Paul prays, "Blessed be the God and Father of our Lord Jesus Christ, the Father of compassion and God of all encouragement, who encourages us in our every affliction, so that we may be able to encourage those who are in any affliction with the encouragement with which we ourselves are encouraged by God" (2 Corinthians 1:3–4). To see behind the loss and sorrow the hand of God is a severe grace.

Did God want Johnny to die? No. God does not want anybody to die. Death is not God's fault. Death is Adam's fault and Eve's fault. Death is the devil's fault. Death is the final enemy, according to St. Paul (1 Corinthians 15:26). Did God know Johnny was going to die when he did? Yes. Why did God allow it? I do not know. Part of being finite and creaturely is to be able to say "I don't know," and accept that fact. The world tries to be God and to know everything. It pressures the Church to explain the unexplainable. But the Church is smarter than the world. She knows what is mystery. In the end, we must trust and surrender. One man sinned and in him all sinned and so all die. Death is the given. One of the great ironies of our civilization is that we live in a culture of death (abortion, suicide, euthanasia, capital punishment) which at the same time denies death and flees from it. We mete out death for others while keeping it at arm's length from ourselves. We all die. The question is not "do we die?" The question is "what happens when we die?" This in turn becomes the question about how we live.

What are we left with at the end of the day? Only this: the Son of God hanging on a cross, his body limp, his voice silent. But in his voluntary humiliation and sacrifice and in the resurrection which is the Father's seal of approval, we see revealed all the love and power of God. This is Christ crucified who is "the power of God and the wisdom of God. For the foolishness of God is wiser than men, and the weakness of God is stronger than men" (1 Corinthians 1:24-25 RSV).

Only in gazing upon the cross can the unanswerable be answered. The answer to the question of suffering and evil is God suffering with us and for us in his Son Jesus Christ. Only by touching in some small, imperfect way the pain of Christ through our own pain, can our pain be accepted and embraced. Only by joining our suffering to his at the foot of the cross may we hope to move beyond it. There is no Easter without Calvary.

TWELVE

A Grief Unveiled

September was approaching. At breakfast a week after we arrived home from Bermuda, Maureen and I were talking about the fact that the children were going back to school in two weeks. We were thinking aloud about the first day of school: the children in their new uniforms, bright and happy and excited to be back with their friends and starting a new year. We said their names: Gregory going into fifth, Thérèse into fourth, David into third, Rose into kindergarten. Then the long pause as we realized we would not see John-Paul with his normal incandescent excitement for all of life's adventures, dressed up in his blue oxford shirt and dark blue slacks with his new bookbag and his hair slicked back. "Ride the wave," Maureen said to me.

Grief is like a wave. It comes rolling in from a far-off place. I could no more push it back than if I were standing in the water at the beach. I could not fight the wave. It moved over me and under me and broke against me, but I could never stop it. It yielded to my presence and in so yielding arrived at its destination. It worked around me. The harder I fought it, the more exhausted I became. So it is with grief. If I tried to fight it, it would vanquish me. If I pushed it down it would stick in my soul and emerge as something else: depression, bitterness, exhaustion.

113

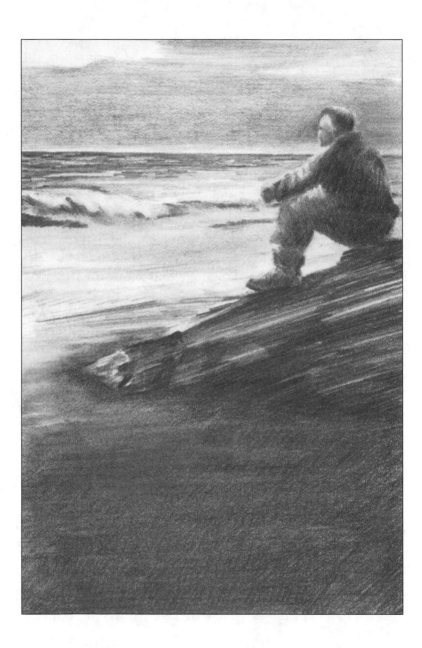

If I yielded to the wave and let it carry me, however, it would take me to a new place. This was what I was discovering five months after Johnny's death. I had to yield to the wave of grief and let it take me. This was a natural process. Grieving took me to high places like the crest of the wave. There were moments of intense emotion that came crashing down around me. It also took me to low places like the lull between waves: moments of remembrance and reflection. It took me to places in my soul that were raw, angry, and hurt, and to others that were like an oasis. Sometimes grief acted as the protagonist, carrying me along in a flood of memories that filled my soul. At other times I was the protagonist, as when I made choices about what I was going to do with my life in light of what had happened to us. The wave spent itself on the shore exhausting itself with each crash and roll. So it was with grief: The more I embraced it, the more I yielded to it, the closer it came to finishing its work.

Yielding to grief. To yield is a posture of vulnerability, of receptivity. That is why most people do not fare too well with it. Vulnerable means "able to be wounded." I had been wounded. If I could not admit this, I was doomed never to move beyond it. The first healing step in the process of grieving, once the initial shock had worn off, was to accept where I was and what had happened to me. I was in grief. It was a place, as real spiritually and psychologically as Athens or Bangkok or Ottawa are physically. Only by accepting this fact could I begin to move. Using the wave analogy, only by yielding to its power and relinquishing control could I come closer to the shore. A swimmer who has been out in a stormy surf comes into shore reeling and tired and battered. Similarly, dealing with grief is exhausting, but not nearly as exhausting as not dealing with it. I was confident that grief embraced would teach me many things. I also knew that if I did not yield, it would ultimately shut down my capacity for life and joy.

Grief strikes at the most unexpected times. Just prior to the beginning of the academic year I had occasion to go over to the school. The first room I went into was the first grade. Johnny would have been in first grade. The desks were neatly set up. Books, place cards, lots of bright shapes and colors. I read the names: Paul and Catherine and Stephen and Genna (Johnny's cousins); Joe, Annie, Andrew, Gregory, Stephanie, Robbie, Walter. These were all the names we had been hearing for the previous three years. Like an earthquake filmed in slow motion, I felt the bricks of my soul coming apart. I tried to find a place to go to escape the pain, but in that moment all that existed was pain and there was no place to go. In such moments I could only hope no one was watching me. I gritted my teeth as hard as I could and told myself, "Not now! Not now! Wait till later, when you're alone." Once again, grief sneaks up from behind. I had not even been thinking about him, and without warning there it was: bone-crunching pain. Even as I thought the emotional pain was beginning to heal, I was once again torn asunder, and I wondered if I had changed at all in five months. But I did notice one thing: These eruptions were less frequent, and they were shorter.

Five months, and I was aware of other changes as well. In a strange way, they may have signaled that I was getting better. While visiting Johnny's grave, seemingly out of nowhere I found myself on my knees, looking at his gravestone, weeping more in anger than in pain. I cried out, "I hate that this happened. This stinks. What are you doing here six feet under? You're supposed to be running around and going to school and jumping on me every morning like you used to." Maybe it was a delayed reaction, but I realized I was angry over what had happened to us. And I cannot say that it was not directed at God. Anger is not necessarily sin, it is emotional information. "Why didn't you prevent this? Why didn't you stop the car? Why did you allow him to be ripped out of our lives? Why have you allowed so much joy to be taken from us?" I say this to God because who else am I going to say this to? In a strange way it is a confession of faith: I am angry because I know you. I am angry because I trust you. I am angry because I love you. But what am I really looking for? I am looking for your fatherly arms to circle round me to quiet my pounding soul.

Despite these moments, or perhaps because of them, I experienced God drawing me to himself as never before. Like the pull of the moon on the tides, I could not resist him. We had loved each other for too long. He was calling to me where the waters lie still, far beneath my emotions. It was to that place deep in my heart where I was absolutely certain that I loved him and he loved me, that he knew what he was about, and that his grace was sufficient for me. In one of these moments of prayer and solitude, another song appeared. It began as the most fundamental statement I could make about Johnny and ended as the most fundamental statement I could make about God. It is a song of joy and hope in the midst of pain, hope that is always deeper than the pain, always the last word, always something about which I harbor absolute certainty. It is a song about heaven. But the new reality, the moment of grace, was the realization that Johnny would be only a small part of the beauty and joy of heaven. Something came back into focus through this song: Johnny's created beauty would point to the uncreated beauty of God.

I Will See You Again

This I know more than I know joy
this I know more than I know pain
this I know more than I know life
that I will see you again

I know more than the sea knows the shore
I know more than the earth knows the rain
I know more than the stars know the sky
that I will see you again

And when I run to touch you and hold you and kiss you
and say that I'm glad it's all over
you say, "Daddy, O Daddy, it's not really over—
in fact it's just really begun."

This I know every tear will run dry
this I know every sorrow will fly
this I know even death will die
and Life will reign on high

And when I settle in for a thousand-year glance
you then point with a motion so fair
you say, "I'm not the one that you really desire
look now—He's right over there."

I see light like a river of fire
I see love like a burning desire
I see Christ with his heart open wide
and his arms outstretched for me

And when dark clouds surround me and waves break upon me
and I feel like closing my door
I say, "Hold on a minute—the time we're together
is more than the time we're apart."

This I know that there is a plan
this I know that I don't understand
this I know that God holds my hand
and he will not let go

So I walk through this valley of tears
but your love drives away all my fears
and I look to the time that draws near
when I will see you again.

The song put together for me the multifaceted reality that I was living. In the secular world, issues of hope, the promise of resurrection, the confident assurance of a future reunion, and eternal life, are regarded with suspicion. If I mentioned those things, people would look at me as if I were masking my grief. They presumed I was out of touch. Such responses pulled me away from the spirituality of death.

But with many Christians, I was pulled away from the humanity of death. I did not know how difficult it would be for those whose theology is more oriented toward the resurrected Christ and his victory over death to appreciate the unfathomable pain of loss, the pressure in my chest that literally made it hard just to breathe sometimes, the unspeakable sorrow that had flooded my heart and mind a million times in those first five months. People wanted me to get on with my life, and I did not want to get on with my life. I wanted to sit with my sorrow. I wanted time alone. I wanted to honor my grief.

And I wanted to be able to speak about Johnny freely. Without anybody saying a word, Maureen and I knew instinctively with whom we could speak about him, and with whom we could not. It was not that some would say, "Stop"; it was rather that their presence did not say, "Speak freely." In such encounters isolation was added to grief. And then we met another parent who had lost a child, and we realized that that parent understood completely, and we did not have to explain a thing. Our treasure was the friends who said, "You can call anytime. If you need to laugh, cry, scream, punch a wall. I will be there for you." Friends like Joe Clemente.

Joe is a big bear of a man, married to Lisa, with five children and at the time two in the womb. We had been neighbors for several years and close friends for many more. Our kids are close in age and great friends with each other. Joe is a physician at Overlook, the hospital to which we had taken Johnny. He had had some time off around Easter, and had taken Lisa and the children to Baltimore for a vacation. They received the call about John-Paul shortly after arriving. They simply got back in the car and drove home. Joe was at my side the minute he arrived home. He has been there ever since. In fact, he hounded me, the way only a good friend can. He had the audacity born of love to say, "Everywhere you look, you're going to see me. I will not let you go through this alone." And so he was almost omnipresent, on the phone if not in person. He sat with me in the car while I wept uncontrollably. He allowed me to see his own acute grief. Joe loved Johnny deeply. In fact, Johnny used to come home and say, "I'm a Clemente. I'm John-Paul Floyd Clemente because Dr. Joe adopted me."

There were others. Men like John Provinsal who was like a great male angel those two days at the hospital—a presence in the background, almost silent. As I walked back and forth, in and out of rooms, talking with doctors, caring for Maureen and the children, I was aware of his presence, as though he felt called to stand sentinel at his post. I could feel strength coming toward me from him, and an incredibly virile tenderness.

These men were but some of the blessings of life in our community. No one had all the wisdom or all the answers. But as Stanley Hauerwas says in his book *Naming the Silences:* "We can't afford to give ourselves explanations for evil when what is required is a community capable of absorbing our grief." This says it perfectly. Whether the community is a family, a church, a covenant community like the one I live in, or a group of friends, the key is the willingness to absorb the pain. In each of the above groups, there were people particularly gifted at doing this. I owe them an eternal debt of gratitude. By their words and their gestures, their love and their presence, they have helped me see that grief is like a tunnel, a passageway, a dark night. It is a process, not a final product; a means, not an end. Joy is the end. Love is the end. Communion is the end. Wrapped in the loving embrace of God is the end. The rest is the journey. I cannot achieve the end without the journey, but the journey is not the end.

Don't grieve like those who have no hope, St. Paul tells us (1 Thessalonians 4:13). I have hope, terribly profound hope, absolute certainty, that Johnny is alive in heaven and that we will be reunited if we live in God's love for the rest of our earthly journey home. Hope is perhaps the greatest gift God has given us to survive this pain. No, I do not grieve without hope. I grieve with hope. I dare to grieve, to let myself feel all the sorrow and pain precisely because I have hope. I can drink the cup to the dregs. I am not afraid to drink it to the dregs. Why? Because Christ rose from the dead. Because he conquered death. By using a double negative ("don't grieve like those who have no hope"), St. Paul is in fact saying, "Grieve." I can let myself go. I can allow myself to feel the pain of separation. I do not have to shut it down or repress it. In fact, I had better not. Why? Because to do so is grieving like those who have no hope. St. Paul is not talking about a psychological condition in which one cannot get out of bed in the morning, where one no longer cares about life or other people. In that case, one needs help to get "unstuck." Rather, he is talking about grieving and letting the gentle hand of Christ lead us through our season of grief.

John-Paul has been received into the loving arms of God. The sacrifice of Christ has assured Johnny a safe passage into everlasting life. The Lord is coming back to take us home. There will be a reunion. We will be together. These are truly words of comfort. They do not say, "Stop grieving." They do not say, "You should be feeling better." They do not say, "Snap out of it." They say, "A better day is coming." And that assurance of a better day has the power to console me in the midst of my pain. We are knit together with Johnny in Christ and in the Church. We are still family, and will be forever.

THIRTEEN

Autumn

September and October saw the summer wane and the autumn blaze forth. I have always loved the early autumn because of its rhythms, smells, and harvest quality. My favorite memory of autumn is from my undergraduate days at Brown University in Providence, Rhode Island. I always left the library at 4:50 P.M. to walk to Mass. At that hour the sky was a color that I called "perfect blue." It is the color of the sky just before the night overtakes the day: dark, but bright. It is found in the backgrounds of the tiny landscapes in the illuminated manuscripts and prayer books of medieval Europe and in the backgrounds of Botticelli's angels. It is flawless. In Providence, it always went hand in hand with yellow leaves and worn brick paths and an almost tactile feeling of happiness. It was a happiness, however, that was more than just the enjoyment of pleasure. It was a joy in the sheer beauty of creation, and with it came the need to give thanks.

I think back to those days every autumn. I remember the crisp, dry smell of the afternoon and the cold feel of a pile of leaves left overnight and the scent of chrysanthemums. Autumn is the crunch of firm apples, the first frosts, the old sweater, and mug of coffee, all of which yield by mid-morning to T-shirts and Frisbees. It is the smoky smell in the neighborhood as the first fires are lit. Autumn is that unique temperature of cold on the surface with warm undertones. Autumn is the height of life, energy, and color prior to the death of winter. It is a visual and symbolic feast, with leaves going out in a blaze of glory, coming down like tongues of fire, showing the world that the last thing they do is the best thing they do: to shine brightly, cause delight, and glorify their Maker.

Nature's changes this year in some ways mirrored the changes in our relationship with John-Paul and our journey through grief. I am not saying that everything started getting better. In fact, things would often get worse before they got better. But the "better" that followed was deeper and more lasting.

I remember clearly a night in early September. I had had perhaps the worst day since the accident. I felt grief with no happy memories, no bright lining—just weight and desolation. I left the house at midnight and was walking up and down the street, praying. It was a cool, starry night. Often on a clear night I will look up and try to imagine heaven. Ever since I was a boy I have imagined that the stars were really holes into heaven and that heaven was the light beyond the darkness. I used to think that if I could get through one of those holes I would be in heaven. I tried to imagine Johnny up there. I do not know if heaven is literally "up there," but since Jesus ascended, the evidence would appear to point in that direction. At one point, I looked up at the stars and cried out, "Johnny, where are you?" Faster than I could draw my next breath, I heard a voice, his voice, say, "Dad, I'm everywhere you are." It was stunning. The timbre, the tone, the accent were his. I stood in my tracks, shoes nailed to the street, as unwilling to move as I was unable. But I felt my heart soaring high above my grief like Icarus on his way to the sun, like Phoenix rising from the ashes, like the Spirit within me drawing me to the Father. I was lost for a moment in the most profound consolation imaginable. So lost in love that the very movement of earth seemed to wait. There was no wind, no sound, no movement. Just the stars and his voice. It was a kiss from my son.

I went home and wrote a love song to Johnny. Of all the songs I have written, this one is my favorite.

Angel in Disguise

Little boy I loved you
about as much as one can love another
In fact it was my only consolation
that now you know how much I loved you

I could not begin to count the many ways you filled our
life with laughter
Old enough to bring us such great joy
but young enough that no dark sorrow crossed your brow
It makes the anguish deeper now

And when I walk the streets at night
or sit by the fire's dying light
or when I'm watching for the dawn
I can almost touch you

There are times when I look up
then I see you standing there before me
The thing I always notice is your smile
and all the light that's in your eyes

Were you an angel in disguise?

And when I walk the streets at night
or sit by the fire's dying light
or when I'm watching for the dawn
I can hear you clearly saying

I am always with you
I am always by your side
I am always with you
I'm everywhere you are.

Earlier that night I had called Maureen (I was away overnight on business). The following morning she was going to support our dear friend Lisa Clemente who was having twins. Maureen said, "It's my first time back in the hospital since Johnny died. When I think of going through those double doors, my stomach does a flip." We prayed together on the phone. That night Maureen had a dream. In the dream, Johnny ran into the kitchen in his plaid shorts and said to her, "Mom, I'm coming with you today." Imagine that—her son "coming" with her to the hospital where he was pronounced dead, coming to help her reach out and support a friend. Apart from Maureen and his grandmothers and aunts, John-Paul knew Lisa better than any other woman. Because the Clementes lived across the street, he was in their house every day playing with David and their son Mike. Johnny was so excited that Lisa was going to have twins. Anyone who knew him knew his extraordinary touch with anyone smaller than himself. It was one of his most striking characteristics.

Later that day, during labor, Lisa started crying. She looked at Maureen and said, "Maureen, he's here—can't you just feel his presence?" The twins were born at 3:55 P.M. and 4:08 P.M., respectively, a boy and a girl. Joe and Lisa named the boy John-Paul.

As I have reflected on these experiences—the voice, the song, the dream, the presence—arranged as they were within a period of twenty-four hours, it struck me that those who are "asleep in the Lord" continue to communicate love and blessings to us. Discrete, yes; subtle, yes; almost imperceptible. But a feeling, nonetheless, of presence, of blessing, of life. I do believe Johnny drew near to us in these experiences. As Maureen said, "I came away missing him but so grateful for his communication."

Did Johnny really speak to me on that cool starry night? Did he really speak to Maureen in her dream? On a literal level, the question is beside the point. The reservoirs of mind, memory, and imagination are gifts of God. They operate under his ordinance. They are open to heavenly influences as well as earthly and demonic ones. For those who love God, everything—mind, memory, imagination, and even grief itself—works to the good. In that sense, I know we were both visited by our son that night.

Several days after the birth of the twins, the boys and I were working in the garage. We were organizing shelves, getting rid of junk, and seeing what we could salvage. Gregory had responsibility for the sports equipment, including ice skates and roller blades. He was matching pairs and putting them in order. When he came upon a pair of red and black ones, he said to me, "Do you want to give these to someone?" "Whose are they?" I asked. "Johnny's." With a motion I can only call visceral, I picked them up and walked out of his view. Then I pressed them—used plastic roller blades—to my face, to smell them—to smell him. Just the smell of small, sweaty feet, but I did it without even thinking.

It was six months since Johnny had died. October 19 would have been his seventh birthday. Maureen and I began talking about how to "celebrate" his birthday. The children always get their favorite meal on their birthdays and baptismal days. Maureen said, "We should probably have pizza and nachos— that was Johnny's favorite meal." We both laughed. She continued, "If he were here he'd be bugging me from now until the 19th about what he wanted for his birthday meal."

Maureen continued, "We should ask the children how they'd like to celebrate Johnny's birthday." "Should we visit the grave?" I asked. "They don't struggle with it as much as we do," Maureen replied. "In fact, the last time we were there I noticed Rosie talking quietly to Johnny while the rest of the children were running around."

Celebrate seems like a funny word to use. But just as nature has its predictable patterns and cycles, I am struck by my own need to ritualize, to commemorate, to remember. This need comes from deep in the human spirit. We received a letter from our parish that week, inviting all the members of the parish who had lost someone in the past year to come to a special memorial Mass on November 2, the feast of All Souls. My immediate reaction was, "I'll move my week around to be there."

Liturgy. Ritual. Sacrament. The life of the Church is like a river flowing from its source to its ultimate surrender in ocean, gulf, or bay. The river carries everything in it and on it toward its destination. Just so the Church—Mother Church—carries us on our journey home. The ancient prayers and gestures, the sameness and solemnity and predictability, are tremendously important spiritually as well as psychologically. Whether we feel dry or not, empty or full, rich or poor, high or low, the prayer of the Church is steady, slow-moving, undistracted, and unperturbed, leading us to our ultimate surrender to God in death.

For the week or two prior to his birthday I had not tried to anticipate what kind of day it would be. The tendency was to think it would be relentlessly awful. But I said to myself, and later to Maureen, "How do I know what kind of day it will be? Maybe it will be extremely difficult, maybe it won't. The only thing we know for sure is that the day belongs to the Lord and we want to live it in a way that honors him." Still, we would feel the surge of emotions and anticipation tugging at our hearts.

How was it? It was hard. It was emotionally draining. It was grace-filled. It was better than I thought it was going to be. We did talk with the children, and together we decided we would go to Mass as a family, buy some flowers, visit his grave, and then go out for hot chocolate. We would let them go to school late. Then at dinner we would eat pizza and nachos and write down all his favorite expressions and the funny things he used to say.

The cemetery was still difficult for Maureen and me. There is nothing as concrete as a grave. It virtually screams: "He is here! He is not with you!" I could not help but think of a lovely, strong little body six feet under. I could not help but think that there is something obscene about the seeming victory of death here—however transitory, however impermanent. I could not help but think how incredibly unnatural it is for parents to bury their children. Maureen wrote a note on the flower card: "Dear John-Paul, we know you're having a great party in heaven today. We love you and miss you. Dad, Mom, Gregory, Thérèse, David, Rose, Susanna, Nicole." Yet despite these reflections, there was grace, that mysterious communication of God's love. The day was like two streams, one of sorrow and the other of love and longing—two streams moving towards their destination in God. Even as moments arose throughout the day that were like a sword in our hearts, moments that took our breath away, they were offset by moments of peace, moments in which we could breathe again, moments in which we could move on to the next thing.

Toward the late afternoon friends started calling and coming over: bringing a rose, a meal, a bouquet, an ice-cream cake for the children. They came with simple words, with hugs and prayers. We are blessed beyond words by our families and our community. There were times we had to leave the table, the room, the desk at the office. But the grace was in being able to return to the table, the room, the desk, and especially in being able to keep on caring for the children, all of whom had their own thoughts and feelings on such a day.

Only by drawing near to grief do I move beyond grief. I was discovering that suffering would not kill me. In a strange way, suffering was becoming a friend, because suffering is connected to love and love is always connected to the cross. I am not talking about the illegitimate suffering we cause ourselves. We need to be careful to determine what is a cross and what is a self-inflicted wound. God wants to redeem and heal our wounds so we can embrace the cross that he has ordained or permitted that we carry.

Maureen and I received two very special gifts on Johnny's birthday. Our friend Pat Weyand called Maureen and told her, "Johnny wants to say 'Thank you.'" And the following letter arrived:

Gregory and Maureen, my dear brother and sister,

For so long I have wanted to express my sympathy, my grief, my deep, deep love for you since John-Paul's "resurrection." That time had not come until now. Our firstborn, Christiana, shares the birthday of John-Paul. As I was reflecting on this last week and praying for you, I was overwhelmed with the sense that John-Paul wanted to thank you, his parents, on this anniversary of his birth. As I sit to write this, all I can picture is our little blonde, blue-eyed boy, red-cheeked, freckled face, bursting forth with an inexhaustible gratitude, jumping up and down singing these words (he can't seem to get the words he so deeply wants to say out fast enough—he is, and I can't emphasize this enough, literally bursting forth with joy and deep, deep gratitude).

"My beloved Mom, my beloved Dad, I am alive, I am alive . . . so fully alive, so perfectly alive. I love you perfectly. Mom and Dad, my love for you is finally perfect and oh is it grand! Far beyond the greatest love earth has ever known. Most precious mother, most precious father . . . thank you, thank you, thank you. I thank you, my Jesus, my almighty King, day and night for having deemed me worthy to be begotten by parents who raised me with eternity in mind. Oh Mom, oh Dad, thank you, thank you.

"Thank you that you prepared me for this eternal glory. Wait until you experience what I am so privileged to know, to see, to hear. I wait for the day when all your questions can be answered and I can hold you ever so tightly. Thank you, thank you that you said 'yes' to my life, that you nurtured me, body, mind, and soul, that you brought me to the waters of baptism where I became a child of our heavenly Father and now am embraced and held by his holy hands. What can I say? Words fail. How can I communicate my gratitude?

"Keep going, Mom and Dad, keep living, Mom and Dad, keep raising my brothers and sisters with a fervent desire for heaven. How worth it life is, Mom and Dad, with all the sorrows, the sufferings, the pains that shall quickly pass and we shall be reunited. I never cease praying for you, nor do I cease thanking my God for the sweet privilege of being begotten in love by you. May my song of gratitude reach your hearts and touch the very core of your souls. You are loved with an everlasting, perfect love. I love you. I love you. I love you."

Gregory and Maureen, I pray you hear these words of resounding love only the way John-Paul could have said it. Our prayers are with you this night.

Love,

Mary Margaret

Later that evening, Maureen and I went out to a talk on *Sudden Loss*. It was given by someone from the Sharing Network, New Jersey's organ and tissue donor organization. Although it seemed crazy to go on Johnny's birthday, we both wanted to. I do not remember too much about the talk. I was not going for the talk. I wanted to be in a room with other people who had lost someone, particularly parents who had lost a child. A kind of solidarity emerges that crosses any boundary—religious, cultural, racial, economic—in meeting another parent who has lost a child. Death is the great leveler. Nobody understands like a bereaved parent. There was a couple there who had lost a 14-year-old boy in a dreadful freak accident. Even in our pain we wanted to reach out and comfort them. Is putting our pain at the service of the other what it means to make up what is lacking in the sufferings of Christ?

There were feelings we could not rush. They needed their own season to come forth and be experienced, acknowledged, lived with, given over to Christ, and offered up with his suffering on the cross. But at the same time we did have hope. And far from being illusory, it was precisely this hope—hope in Christ, the hope of eternal life, the hope of a future encounter—that allowed us to experience the separation in all its awful depth. We could look horror in the face because it was not forever. We could drink the cup of suffering to the dregs because we knew that one day Christ would fill our cup with the new wine of the resurrection. Hope kept turning our gaze toward Christ.

Shortly after Johnny's birthday Maureen and I went down to the shore for the weekend. It is almost impossible to find the time to be alone or quiet when there are six children running around the house. It was a gift just to watch the sky and the ocean, the waves and the sand, to walk the beach, to sit quietly. The silence and the big, elemental forms of nature help the soul regain its bearings. Even in the midst of pain I knew we were getting better. It is true: The pain diminishes. Such is the transcendent life force within us because we are created in his image and he is life (John 14:6). Even when a dark wave approached we could say, "I've seen this wave before, and it didn't crush me. Took me for a ride? Sure. Knocked me on my face? Yes. Crushed me? No. Why? Because Life is in me."

The process of healing is an exquisite interplay of grace and nature. It had been six months since Johnny's death, and I did not think of him every hour. I thought of him every day and I could not imagine going a day without thinking about him, but I did not think of him every hour. It had been six months, and we were experiencing moments of joy, grace, and laughter as a couple and a family. The immanent life force which is Christ himself kept on bursting through. The confident hope of seeing Johnny again was like the air we breathe. There were moments in which all I could do was bow my head in gratitude to God for his love and mercy toward us.

During the month of October I heard the following passage read at church: The LORD ". . . is a God of justice, / who knows no favorites. / Though not unduly partial toward the weak,/ yet he hears the cry of the oppressed. / He is not deaf to the wail of the orphan, / nor to the widow when she pours out her complaint. / . . . He who serves God willingly is heard; / his petition reaches the heavens. / The prayer of the lowly pierces the clouds; / it does not rest till it reaches its goal, / Nor will it withdraw till the Most High responds, / judges justly and affirms the right" (Sirach 35:12–14, 16–18).

The Lord hears the cry of the oppressed. He is not deaf to the wail of the orphan. The prayer of the lowly pierces the clouds. It does not withdraw till the Most High responds. The psalmist continues the theme: "When the just cry out, the LORD hears / and rescues them from all distress. / The LORD is close to the brokenhearted, / saves those whose spirit is crushed" (Psalm 34:18–19).

I asked myself *What has changed here?* I had heard, read, and sung these lines a hundred times before. The answer was this: I had changed. I used to read these lines and they were about other people. Now I read them and said, "This is me!" The Word of God was talking about me. The Word of God was speaking to me. I resonated with these words and they moved me deeply.

Yes, I am oppressed. I wail. I am poor and in distress. I am brokenhearted. It is my spirit that is crushed. These sacred words describe the depth of the human heart, and that is one reason why they are sacred. Whatever touches the human heart at its depths is sacred. I realized that God was looking at me when he inspired the psalmist to write. This word ever ancient and ever new made me understand that I am not alone. Not alone: It is the alienation added to the suffering that pushes many over the edge. God had not left me alone. In these readings I saw I was one with most of humanity, humanity that experiences poverty, distress, broken-heartedness. I no longer go to serve the poor. I have become the poor.

But I am not alone, and I am understood. Allowing myself to be drawn into this unfathomable presence, this compassionate understanding, was part of the healing. It was living in the presence of God, with or without the answers I thought I needed.

Perhaps I was coming to understand the cross. The author of the Epistle to the Hebrews states plainly that Jesus endured the cross for the joy that was set before him (Hebrews 12:2). The pattern is archetypal: the hero enduring enormous pain and suffering in the quest of his beloved. But here we have no mere archetype from the realms of mythology. Here is the Son of God, Creator and Redeemer of the very people who are abusing and reviling him, falling under blows and curses that tear at his heart even more than they tear at his flesh. And what does he do?

He endures in silence. He endures the cross, "despising its shame." The shame of the cross was its ignominy. It was reserved for the dregs of society and meant as a warning to anarchists, rabble-rousers, and the like. Jesus despised its shame for the joy that was set before him. What was that joy? I think it was the joy of opening heaven to all who would call upon his name. The joy of seeing countless throngs safe at home in his Father's house in a life that never ends, and the joy of being eternally in his Father's presence as God and man: These joys were worth every pain.

We are told in this passage to keep our eyes fixed on Jesus. Fixed means "locked on," "gazing upon." The key is to keep looking at Jesus. Is it possible that all wisdom could be reduced to this: to gaze on Christ crucified until we are moved by love to sorrow and contrition? To gaze on his passion until we know we are unconditionally loved? To gaze on him until we notice the object of his gaze? And what was the object of his gaze? Where were his eyes fixed as he endured this torment? I suspect on two places: on his Father and on the world.

On his Father: The only begotten Son who is one with the Father was not looking at a God who had turned away from him. Jesus is always in love with his Father. The eyes of his heart are fixed, securely fastened, on his Father. Securely fastened on the Love that has allowed, permitted, demanded this sacrifice so that one man's agony could be the eternal joy of all who come to God through him.

And his eyes were fixed on the world: He looked out on the uncountable generations of broken humanity that would be healed by his wounds. He looked out in sorrow on all those who would reject his offer of mercy and forgiveness and looked out with joy on all who would say yes. His gaze moved back and forth, offering the world to his Father and his Father to the world.

When my eyes are fixed on Jesus and I can feel him and hear him call out to me, I can endure the pain of separation. The pain of separation hurts tremendously. As Bishop Magee, a close friend and spiritual mentor from our time in Ireland, wrote in a letter to us, "The pain will never be fully healed until you see John-Paul again." But yoked with Christ, I can endure this cross.

The cross casts its shadow over the life of everyone. Heaven is not reached except through the cross. He who said, "I am the way . . . follow me," ascended the cross. To reach heaven is to carry the cross and then to be lifted up on it, whether now or later. God does not rejoice in our suffering, but he allows it and in the mystery of his plan uses it to bring about a greater good and to release more love in the world.

Love and suffering: Like the rose around the briar, they are entwined on this earth. There is no great love without great suffering, at least not until the end of time, when love will swallow up suffering even more surely than the earth swallowed the body of John-Paul.

I stare at the cloud that separates the mind of God from the mind of humanity. Saints and mystics penetrate it occasionally. But in a way that I do not yet understand, God turns everything around. In the end, all our pain and suffering is turned around. What I discover, again and again, is that God's ways are not my ways. But I can love him and trust him without understanding him.

When I keep my mind "stayed" on Christ, on the person of Jesus who loved me and died for me and promises me eternal life where every tear will be wiped away and every sorrow destroyed—when I keep my mind stayed on him, I can think with more of an eternal perspective. I am reminded of the shortness of this life in relation to eternity. This concept helps me to think that compared to the time we will have together in heaven, this temporary separation, as excruciating as it is, is nonetheless temporary.

Scripture records Christ's resurrection appearance to Mary Magdalene. "And they [the angels] said to her, 'Woman, why are you weeping?' She said to them, 'They have taken my Lord, and I don't know where they laid him.' When she had said this, she turned around and saw Jesus there, but did not know it was Jesus" (John 20:13–14). She did not know it was Jesus, presumably because of his glorified body. In fact she did not know him until he called her name: "Mary." What a commentary! I am known when my name is spoken. And when my name is spoken by God, I am born again. Yet Christ says to her, "Do not hold onto me." This spoke to me forcefully about Johnny.

I could not hold onto John-Paul any more than Mary Magdalene could hold onto Jesus. The order of things had changed for her and so it had for me. *Do not hold onto me.* What did this mean for me as it relates to John-Paul? *Do not rely on the way you used to relate to me, but open yourself to a new way of relating to me: more subtle, more discreet.* This way of relating is difficult, yes, without the body to touch, because we express love physically through touch. That part is gone, until the resurrection of the body. There is no minimizing the enormity of that loss. The relationship is not as before. But even more important, I must affirm that the relationship continues. It is changed, made into something different. It is nonetheless a relationship, continued in the spirit, in prayer, and in the Church.

FOURTEEN

Joy to the World

It was cold. The leaves had fallen, the frosts had come, the earth was hard. The children were bundled up when they went out. The car rarely heated up before we had arrived at our destination, and the tile floor in the bathroom was always cold to the touch. The "perfect blue" of the autumn sky was now black, while the days themselves were often gray and strung out like sheets on the line.

For All Saints Day (November 1), Gregory had to write an essay. The students were told they could choose to write about any saint they wanted. He chose his brother.

Saint John-Paul

To begin with most saints didn't like pizza. But then again we're not talking about any ordinary saint. We're talking about Saint John-Paul.

Saint John was born October 19, 1988. Saint John had quite an interesting life. He was a missionary three times in six and a half years. The first time John was a missionary he moved from the United States to Ireland with his family at the age of two. During his time there he brought light and happiness to all he met. When John was four he went to do missionary work in Appalachia. He would play with the children at the Bible School we started there. One time one of his friends caught a lizard crawling up his sleeping bag. Saint John's most recent work was with my Dad, my brother, and me with the Penobscot tribe in Maine. He helped bring the children closer to Jesus and brought joy to the whole camp.

As you can see, Saint John-Paul led a very unusual life. Saint John-Paul at the age of six was hit by a car and killed. Through his death he has brought many people back to the church and the Holy Eucharist.

November was also the month in which we finally got around to ordering a gravestone.

I remember standing in the kitchen with Maureen while she was making dinner, asking her what words she wanted on his grave. We kept choking on the words. We finally admitted we could not even believe we were having the discussion about our six-year-old son. We managed to get through the "beloved son" kinds of epitaphs, none of which was satisfactory. I said to Maureen, "I want something from Scripture that's going to ring out the truth of what's really going on here. I want something that's going to tell me the truth, and hopefully tell the truth to everyone who visits his grave or just passes by." We decided on the following line from St. John's Gospel:

I will see you again and your hearts will be full of joy.
(John 16:22 NJB)

The literal meaning refers to the resurrection of the Lord. I do not think we were stretching the text too far to say that it also refers to all who have died in the Lord. I hear Johnny say it to me every time I visit his grave.

In November, Maureen and I started talking about Christmas. Parents with a large family have to begin speaking about Christmas early, in order to address the seemingly end-less details of who is coming and who is going where, what the children need and what the children want. Beyond that is the spiritual dimension of how we can prepare to celebrate so great a feast as the coming among us of God as man. All this takes some preparation.

During our first conversation Maureen said, "I think about Christmas, how much fun it will be for the children and how I'm looking forward to it. Then a wave of grief comes over me and I realize my heart is still broken." I knew what she was talking about—one moment everything was fine, and the next a legs-cut-out-from-under-you feeling that seemed to come from nowhere.

The first thing we decided was to stay home instead of going to my parents' or Maureen's parents'. For one thing, we had just discovered that Maureen was pregnant. We were shocked and thrilled, though Maureen was at this point more shocked than thrilled. "It's not the baby," she explained. "I love the baby. It's just the pregnancy—the sickness and exhaustion on top of everything else." "Sickness" is an understatement. With Nicole, Maureen lost twelve pounds in the first three months and became dehydrated because she was vomiting up to five times a day. During one particularly "green" moment she said to me, "Whoever coined the term 'morning sickness' must have been a man because it lasts all day!" And before the pregnancy with Nicole was the delivery of Susanna, who had the umbilical cord wrapped around her neck three times. The consequence of this situation was that anytime Maureen pushed, the flow of oxygen to Susanna would be severely constricted. Our obstetrician, Dr. Abu Alam, who is a pro-life Muslim, performed a high-forceps delivery without anesthesia. "Pain!" Maureen recounted later. "You don't know the meaning of the word!" Susanna was born gray-blue and breathing with difficulty. Maureen barely had time to greet her before she was whisked away to the neonatal intensive care unit. When Susanna was out of danger, Dr. Alam said to us, "All I can tell you is that God wanted that baby alive." He then went on to recount that five months earlier he had confronted the same situation, and that baby had died. Susanna is fine, healthy, and happy. We named her after the biblical Susanna (Daniel 13) because God delivered both of them out of impossible situations. While it is true that a woman after childbirth "no longer remembers the pain because of her joy that a child has been born into the world" (John 16:21), nonetheless, the entire mosaic of bright and dark moments flowed back into Maureen's mind and emotions as she thought "I am pregnant" and tried to adjust to that fact.

Maureen's pregnancy was the first reason we decided to stay home. But the other reason was simply that Christmas was the next event added to all the others in this year of "firsts." No one plans the year of firsts. It was not until a few had happened—summer vacation, the start of school, or Johnny's birthday—that we realized we would have to confront many more. The more the family celebrates, the more "firsts" they will encounter. There are the big events one anticipates: Christmas, Easter, birthdays, sacraments. Different from these are the many less public moments, moments that bring vividly to mind just how large the absence is. Moments like Rose coming into the kitchen the morning after the funeral and asking, "Where's Johnny?"

After much conversation we decided to invite both of our extended families for Christmas dinner, including whatever aunts, uncles, and cousins wanted to come. Left to ourselves, we might have skipped the festivities altogether. We realized, however, that for the sake of the children we needed to let the day flow as naturally as possible. They had a right to such a celebration, and we would have to find a more private time for our own thoughts and feelings.

Toward mid-November I took the day off and we went Christmas shopping. It was great to have this time alone with Maureen. It is a tradition we have had since the beginning of our marriage: we go to Mass and then combine coffee, lunch, and shopping for the children. It is a day for which we plan and have always enjoyed. The tradition also helps to prevent the season of Advent from disappearing in the blur of the Christmas rush. We relish the time. But at one point I looked at Maureen in the aisle of the toy store. She was weeping as she looked at the toys for a boy who was not there. I embraced her and knew that even in the midst of a busy and happy day the moments of pain would never fail to surprise us: everything is fine, and then in a moment everything is changed.

We had no plans for Thanksgiving. We probably would have played our annual football game with the Clementes in the morning and had dinner as a family in the afternoon but for a phone call we received from Bob and Eileen Filoramo. Eileen and I have been friends ever since college. I brought her to visit our church community during winter break one year. She ended up moving down after graduation, marrying my friend Bill Longo, and having a family. When their third daughter Margaret was ten months old, Bill died of leukemia at the age of 32. In another part of New Jersey at the time, Bob Filoramo was caring for his wife, Nancy, who was dying of cancer, while also taking care of his four children and running the English department of a large suburban high school. Both the Longos and the Filoramos were part of our community and knew each other. Eventually, Bob and Eileen married, blending their families and having several more children together. They are no strangers to suffering. They called and said, "Come on over. Stay as long as you like." As it turned out, it was one of the best Thanksgivings ever, clearly expressed in the greatest gift of all: friendship.

In December I realized that I had stopped thinking in terms of weeks since the accident. The holiday celebrations were themselves complex and tiring, even without the sadness of grief. But this shift in thinking implied a relinquishing, a not holding on so fiercely to the day of his death. It was another small sign of healing. December 1 was Maureen's baptismal day. We honored her at dinner. I gave her "Johnny's Mother," a poem I had written three months after Johnny died.

Johnny's Mother

She lives on the cross, amidst nightly feedings and laundry
Nicole's cries and Susanna's cries
everywhere and nowhere she sees him
her knees hurt from carrying children
upstairs and downstairs
day after day.

She lives on the cross, her heart pierced
by a lance as long as life
and still she leans into her work
with strong back and strong arms
playing with the children, wrapping gifts,
making cards that say I love you, and
taking time with her daughters and sons.

She lives on the cross, dropping on the bed each night exhausted
too tired to think she asks
what has happened to us and
how will I live without him
She looks at God and God looks at her
in the silence.

She lives on the cross and yet she knows deep down
that this is not the end of us or her or him.
She can raise her fist against death because
she loves the Christ who walked
out of the tomb with her boy's name
written on his hand.

After dinner we asked the children how they wanted to remember John-Paul this Christmas. Shy and retiring as they are, they were full of ideas! In the clatter of voices, all competing simultaneously, I heard them say: "Let's replant the tree and the rosebush by his grave. Let's make a grave blanket for his grave. Let's put petitions in John-Paul's stocking. Let's make a Christmas tree out of pictures of John-Paul. Why don't we plant a Christmas tree on Johnny's grave and make an ornament of a picture of John-Paul?" Then one said quietly, "Why don't we ask Johnny for a specific Christmas gift that he could personally ask Jesus to send us?" It was amazing to see how effortlessly the children considered Johnny part of the family. Sometimes it was as though he was in another room, so near was he to them.

Advent is a season of waiting, of prayerful preparation, of quiet, of hope. It is one of my favorite seasons because all the readings from the Old and New Testaments point to redemption, salvation, fulfillment. While we waited in hope, God was busy at work digging around with the spade of his grace in ways we could not have imagined. One episode with Thérèse stands out in my mind.

In the middle of December Thérèse woke up screaming. She was having a nightmare in which Maureen was dying of cancer. Running into her room, I hugged her and held her closely until she quieted down, telling her I was there and Mommy was okay and it was just a bad dream. When she finally fell back asleep I climbed back into bed. With a parent's intuition I told Maureen the dream came from Thérèse's subconscious dealing with repressed grief.

The next day I talked to Thérèse about her nightmare. "Do you know why you had that nightmare?" "No." "I think I know why. I think you had that nightmare because deep down inside a very real part of you is trying to help you with your feelings about the accident and about Johnny's death so they can't stay in there and frighten you." Whispering a prayer for help, I continued. "Thérèse, I think you haven't been able to admit how bad it was to see your brothers on the lawn and to stand there as the ambulances whisked them away with people running around and police sirens screaming. Your body and your mind are telling you in different ways how bad it was. They use other pictures and other pains to let you know. The reason they do this is very simple: so you can admit what happened and accept it. You don't need to deny a single thing about this tragedy and how it affected you.

"Another thing. You need everything to be okay for others and you try to make everything okay. But you know what, Thérèse? This isn't okay and it's never going to be fully okay until Jesus comes again and you see Johnny. It's okay for it not to be okay. It's okay to be angry and hurt and upset and sad."

It was a breakthrough moment. As in other breakthrough moments I have had with Thérèse, her eyes filled up with tears, because by God's grace I was touching her spirit. Her voice got very soft and her spirit got very soft and once again she became a little girl who wanted nothing more than the love and protection of a father.

I realized as I spoke to her that I was speaking to myself. I could not make this better. I could not wave a magic wand and take away the pain—not for myself, my family, or the man who hit the boys. I needed to accept this. It was a moment that was at once mutually revelatory and self-revelatory. I knew I would get better. Healing the pain, the memories, and the trauma, however, is a job only God can do. My job was to pray that I would not miss these moments when God is at work. My job was to lead the children through these moments—to press, but not too hard; to assure them they are getting through this and growing through this and they will not only survive this but will thrive. This is my vocation as their father—and to trust that all shall be well.

A few days before Christmas we made a grave blanket for Johnny. I told the children they could stick their favorite things on it. We took it to the cemetery on December 23. On Christmas Eve, J.J. and Nancy offered to take the children for a few hours so Maureen and I could have some time alone to pray, talk, and visit the grave. They bought them special gifts and had a little Christmas Eve party for them. Maureen and I sat at a diner, able to speak to each other without the constant interruptions that were part of daily life. When we finished our coffee, we went to the cemetery. We hiked through the snow to his marker: John-Paul Floyd 1988–1995. The stone had not yet arrived because of the inclement weather.

There we stood, silently, our arms around each other, praying quietly. After a while we visited the graves of some other friends of ours and then went home. When we arrived at the house, I said to Maureen, "Sit down. I want to give you one gift early. The other gifts are gifts, this one is a treasure." It was a book called "*Yes! John-Paul Floyd.*" "Yes!" was Johnny's most enthusiastic response to life. My sister-in-law Debbie put it together for me. It was a book of photos from the six-and-a-half years of his life. What made it so special?

Three weeks after Johnny died I was cleaning my office. My wastepaper basket was chock full, so I began lifting the paper out of it, sheaf by sheaf. Halfway through the basket I came upon almost thirty pages of John-Paul's schoolwork: coloring, writing, projects from kindergarten. What would normally have warranted scant attention now seemed like a great gift: all these things that he had made with his own mind and hands. I went through them and put them in a closet with some of his other belongings. Later I had the idea to use them as the pages of a book, with the photos superimposed upon them.

We sat on the couch looking at this beautiful handmade book about our son, joy and pain locked in a passionate embrace. "Boy," I said, "this hurts like hell, doesn't it?" "Yes," Maureen answered softly, "but hell lasts forever."

On Christmas Eve we went to the vigil together as a family. The vigil always begins with caroling. Just as different verses of Scripture had struck me forcefully over the past months, so the words of the Christmas carols brought vividly to mind the truth and beauty of this season.

> No more let sin and sorrow grow,
> Nor thorns infest the ground;
> He comes to make his blessings flow

Far as the curse is found,
Far as the curse is found,
Far as, far as the curse is found.

("Joy to the World," verse 3)

The curse is death, and no one escapes it. Death entered the world through the envy of the devil, the disobedience of our first parents, and all the personal acts of disobedience that flow from that primordial one. In the midst of the curse, however, Christ came. Christmas is the birth of hope. Christ had to take on our flesh before he could take away the sin of the world in that flesh. In the songs and symbols, in the consecration of bread and wine into the Body and Blood of the Lord, in the community of believers, my hope was renewed. Even if shot through with pain and memory, my hope was renewed.

On Christmas Day many from both our families came over. Their presence provided a good distraction. We had the morning alone with the children, and we lit candles, processed around the house, put baby Jesus in the manger, and sang songs. It was an act of obedience to sing songs of joy. The psalmist cries out: " . . . give to the LORD the glory due his name" (Psalm 96:8). There is a duty required that goes beyond our emotions. But the fruit of obedience is freedom. On Christmas Day, eight months after Johnny died, Maureen and I shared food and drink, fellowship with family and friends, laughter and tears, fun times with the children, and intimate moments with each other. The time was rich and graced. And it was about to change dramatically.

On St. Stephen's Day, the day after Christmas, Maureen started bleeding—just a bit of spotting to start with. I thought maybe she needed to put up her feet and rest. But the bleeding continued. Once again we were caught in a situation which was completely out of our control. Once again we were confronted with a God whose ways we did not understand. In the season of the birth of a child, we were losing a child.

The following night I was praying over the baby in her womb as we went to bed. "You're not in denial about this, are you?" Maureen asked. "What do you want me to do?" I retorted. "Pray that the baby dies?" "No," she said, "I just want you to be prepared for what's going on here." I prayed that God would protect the life of this child. I said, "Come on, Lord, not two deaths in one year." The next day we went to the doctor. He looked at the sonogram and said, "See, there's the sac. There's no baby in the sac. I'm so sorry."

As we were driving away Maureen said to me, "How are you doing?" I replied, "I don't think I have any emotions left." This was our third miscarriage. It was the feast of the Holy Innocents so we named him Innocent. He joined Francis and Hope, our two other children who died in the womb. Maureen knew early on that something was not right. She was not sick and she was not exhausted. She had been preparing her spirit all along. As for myself, I still had to say to God, "Are you trying to make this year as hard as you possibly can?" before I could surrender.

On New Year's Eve, Maureen was in bed praying, trying to surrender the year that was ending and asking for an increase of trust for the year to come. She opened the Scriptures and came upon the famous passage from Romans: "I consider that the sufferings of this present time are as nothing compared with the glory to be revealed for us" (Romans 8:18). The glory to be revealed must be utterly astonishing if it renders the sufferings that preceded it as "nothing." I cannot say these sufferings are nothing, and neither does St. Paul. He simply states that compared to the unveiled presence of God they will be as nothing. They will be eclipsed by his infinite power and majesty and mercy and tenderness. For me, the reality of his presence, however veiled, is manifest in the will to go on: to go on being a husband and a father. To go on praying. To go on proclaiming that his mercies never end. The reality of his presence means that I am moved by a power not my own to love God and to continue to surrender to him. And the fruit of that surrender, dare I say it, is joy. Joy to the world, the Lord is come.

FIFTEEN

Light from the Cross

I told a friend that one day I would write an essay called "On the Suspension of Understanding as a Prerequisite for the Spiritual Life." The comment was only partly ironic. The scholastic theologians of the Middle Ages expounded the theological maxim *fides quaerens intellectum* (faith seeking understanding). They were smart enough to realize, however, that faith guides one surely through the night precisely when understanding ends.

In John's Gospel Jesus says: "What I am doing, you do not understand now, but you will understand later" (John 13:7). He is speaking to Peter as he bends down to wash Peter's feet. He is also speaking to me. I do not know what he is doing through Johnny's death. I do not understand why it happened. I do not know how God is working it to the good, as he promises he will (Romans 8:28). Sometimes I envision a tapestry woven of the strands of Johnny's life and death and the strands of our suffering. These strands are tied to others, like hands reaching out in the darkness where they touch the lives of others and draw them into his merciful embrace. I envision the strands but I do not see them. I hope that they are real. I hope that God will permit us not to waste this suffering. I hope that suffering embraced might become true compassion.

" . . . later you will understand." This, too, is my hope: that what I now see sometimes through a glass darkly and sometimes not at all, I shall later see in the fullness of light. And then, in the revelation of God, I will either understand or not care to understand. But whether the understanding comes or is forgotten in the ecstasy of heaven's first kiss, it will not matter. Then, there will be only joy.

Understanding is like a light turned on in a darkened room, or like the dawn that enables one to see things as they really are. We speak of being enlightened when confusion yields to clarity or ignorance yields knowledge. I am coming to see, as never before, that the true light, the uncreated light, the light that gives life, comes from the cross. The elements of the natural world must receive light in order to shine forth and dazzle us with their beauty. But the cross—the cross emanates light and enlightens everything that its shadow touches. Light comes from the cross: a simple realization, to be sure. Simple, as all the deep things of life are simple. The cross, icon of all that is hateful and diabolical, is transformed by him who willingly, lovingly, passionately, ascended it. On the cross, love is revealed as sacrifice. When I gaze on the cross, when I ponder Christ's suffering, death, and resurrection, when I fix my inward eye upon him, I am drawn out of myself. My vision becomes clearer and my hope grows stronger.

It was February. As the dark winter months drew on and the earth itself seemed asleep in death, I noticed that grief changes with time. There is a difference between early grief and later grief. Early grief is acute; later grief is more diffuse. Early grief smacks, stings, punches; later grief is more gentle. Early grief is a stalker; later grief is a companion. Early grief consists of crags and crevices; later grief, of furrows softened by the passage of time.

When does the transition come from one to the other? There is no definitive time line. One cannot tell another, "You will suffer acute grief for two months and then move on to the next phase." While the element of time is important, the passage from one kind of grief to another has more to do with acceptance and surrender. As the new year began, I could see signs of growth.

Maureen and I watched the children closely over these ten months, trying to do everything that grace and common sense inspired us to do to make our home a place in which they could grieve and grow. We wanted it to be a place where they were encouraged to share their thoughts and express their feelings, a place where they knew they could interrupt us at any time if they needed to talk about Johnny, a place where they did not have to protect the grown-ups. We tried to make our home a place where they could learn about themselves, about God, and about life through the prism of Johnny's death, a place where they could become whole. We wanted to express to them in the clearest language possible that nothing was more important in this season of their lives than working through their experience of Johnny's death.

How much the children were willing and able to speak was and continues to be sensitive territory. While they were very free to remember and speak about John-Paul's life, they were more hesitant to talk about how they were reacting to his death and the impact of his absence in their lives. This is understandable—most children do not have to confront the death of a sibling. They frequently had to deal with emotions that are not normally part of children's everyday experience (at least not as intensely or persistently). At the beginning, our conversations with the children needed no form—they just came out. A few months down the road we began to incorporate such conversations into our weekly meetings with the children. These times gave them a structured space in which they could talk about Johnny, as well as the more spontaneous moments. Both were helpful.

One evening I asked Thérèse to take me step by step through what she had seen at the accident. She talked about the police cars, the ambulances, and worst of all, her brothers on the lawn. In the rush of activity, I never noticed that she had come outside with Nicole. In fact, she was the third person on the scene. Although she seemed to "recover" quickly, I knew many more feelings were unresolved than resolved. She told me that at night scary thoughts came back to her and made it hard for her to go to sleep. I prayed with her and we asked the Lord to take the fear out of her heart. I suspected we would be returning to this prayer many times. Once again I witnessed the grace of dialogue overcoming isolation.

This conversation, which enabled Thérèse to know that she was not alone, was followed by one that did the same for me. In January, I was away with the leaders of our community. During one particular time of prayer, I was lying prostrate with my face on the floor. I had just said to the Lord, "Something new needs to happen here." I meant it in terms of my relationship with God and with John-Paul. "I am tired of the grief, the heaviness, the loneliness, the longing, the ache in my heart." Just then someone tapped me on the shoulder. It was my friend Ed Greey. He bent down and said, "Can I talk to you?"

I got up and followed him into the kitchen. Ed is a big, strong, man's man kind of guy—camping, fly-fishing, a genius with his hands. He was crying. No, he was weeping intensely. He put his hands on my shoulders and said through his tears, "I don't know what's happening here. All I know is that God has given me a burden for you—I feel the weight of the grief and sorrow you've been carrying these months. And I think God wants me to tell you that he wants to lift it—the grief and the sorrow—and give you joy. And, Gregory, he wants you to know how much he loves you."

That was it. There were the two of us, standing in the kitchen, embracing one another and weeping. As I think of it I am reminded of an amazing line of poetry I heard years ago while driving in the car:

> There must be men among whom we can cry
> And still be counted as warriors.

But in that strong, manly embrace, and in those tears of a brother sharing my grief and pain, and those kind and tender words, something happened. I experienced God saying to me, "I know how much this hurts, and I am with you." And I knew that God was embracing me through Ed and that that embrace was lifting some of the pain. True, the healing comes from heaven. But how often heaven appears in the heart of a friend.

As the winter moved on, the joy of Christmas with its celebration of birth yielded to the solemnity of Lent and its commemoration of suffering and death. Lent is the liturgical season during which Christians remember Christ's forty days in the desert fasting, praying, and resisting the devil. It is a time when the Church joins with the Lord in imitation of his sacrifice and prayer. During this time, other lights came to us, other grace notes. The most stunning of them happened in February while I was on a Lenten retreat with the men of the community. I had decided to do a vigil from 1:00 A.M. to 2:00 A.M. I had brought the Stations of the Cross with me to secure a focus to my prayer. The Stations of the Cross are a series of scripturally based meditations on Christ's journey from Gethsemane to Calvary. They trace the principal events of the last hours of his life. I had a copy that was written by St. Alphonsus, a great eighteenth-century preacher from Italy. Though I thought I would move prayerfully through them all, I never got past the Second Station, entitled "Jesus is led to the Cross." St. Alphonsus writes: "Jesus saw the cross. He kissed the cross. He embraced the cross. He received the cross joyfully from the Father's hands." I stopped. He saw the cross, kissed the cross, embraced the cross. Those I could at least imagine. "He received it joyfully from the Father's hands." I said to the Lord: "I am not there yet."

As I pondered these words I grew aware of the presence of the Lord. It was the kind of awareness in which time and space seem to disappear, in which one is no longer conscious of walls and ceilings, the presence of others, or the passage of time. It was the kind of time as blessed as it is rare, where one knows only God. As I drank in this moment of profound stillness, I heard his wordless voice: "This is a gift. Everything that has happened to you is a gift." I decided to try the thought on for size without committing myself to it: "This is a gift." I tried it on like a hat to see if it fit. And having tried it on, I could not get it off. "This is a gift. A gift for you, a gift for Maureen. A gift for the children. A gift for the community and the Church."

I was rocked by this, rocked by the prospect that this may have been God speaking. The words made me tremble inside. More than rocked, I was overwhelmed. I became aware that I needed a whole new way of thinking if I were even to consider taking this as a word from the Lord. *Could it be that God is inviting me to unite my sufferings with his suffering for the redemption of the world?* The concept sounded very big. I felt very small. The next morning at breakfast I tried to share what had happened.

But I could hardly talk. The experience seemed to grow and become larger in me. During prayer I went outside with J.J. I stood in the parking lot with him for twenty minutes, unable to talk, trying to take in the word I felt was from God. Then J.J. told me an amazing story. "Gregory," he said, "ten minutes before you came up to me, Johnny came to me in a vision and said, 'Uncle John, I'm okay, I'm really okay.'"

I went home later in the day to tell Maureen what had happened. She told me that in prayer that very morning God had said to her, "John-Paul sits on my lap. And just like he used to pester you when he wanted something, that's what he does to me. All day long he tells me everything you need—you, his parents that he loves so much. And I tell you, I am going to richly bless you." What can one do with moments like these except to bow one's head?

The following week Maureen made a retreat with the women of the community. As God had been intimately present to me, he was equally so to her. At the end of the weekend she went to the microphone to share her highlight.

"I had a great expectancy that the Lord was going to do something for me this weekend," she began. "What I felt I needed the Lord to do was to restore my trust in him. I have not done it perfectly, but I've tried to serve the Lord and to give my life to him as best I can. I felt that I put all my eggs in a basket and the Lord let it drop. I had to say this to the Lord, because even though my mind knows the truth, my heart was broken, and my heart was very fearful of being vulnerable to the Lord because I felt like he wasn't faithful to me. He allowed something very tragic to happen, something I didn't think he ever would." She paused, gathering her thoughts, looking out at the faces of so many women who had loved her through these months.

"As the retreat began, I opened Scripture and read from Psalm 37, the psalm that was engraved on our wedding invitation: 'Trust in the LORD and do good / that you may dwell in the land and live secure. / Find your delight in the LORD / who will give you your heart's desires [verses 3 and 4].' This was God's word for me, coming into the weekend. On Friday night I went to the vigil. I needed time alone with the Lord, time to be alone with my grief, time to vent. I needed time to express all this to the Lord, because at home it tends to come in bits and pieces. As I sat before the Blessed Sacrament, the only thing I heard the Lord say in my heart, over and over again, was 'Maureen, John-Paul is alive! Maureen, John-Paul is alive!' Over and over and over again. It may sound like a very simple thing, but God wanted to assure me that John-Paul was alive." The room was silent as Maureen continued to speak.

"Saturday morning as I went to prayer I began again to express my grief to the Lord. All I could say to him was, 'Lord, my mind knows I should trust you, but my heart is not there, and all I can say is "help."' And then I heard these words: 'I will tell you this: I asked the very same thing of my mother that I have asked of you. How can you consider that a disfavor in your life, if what I asked of Mary, I have asked of you?' I read the passage of Jesus in the Garden of Gethsemane. Jesus said, 'Father, if it be your will take this cup away from me.' Gregory and I prayed this prayer many times in the hospital. But the Father required of Jesus his life. I had a sense of the Lord saying to me, 'If I asked Mary to give her son and I asked Jesus to give his life, it is a mystery, but it is a favor, a spiritual favor, this cross in your life.' I wept a lot and experienced a lot of healing. I experienced the Blessed Mother at John's deathbed; I experienced her as I held his lifeless body in my arms, but I never experienced her like I did yesterday. The Lord told me to put everything in her mantle and walk with her to the foot of the cross, and together Mary and Jesus and I could go to the Father and offer what he has asked of all of us—*his* will, back to him. The other thing I sensed the Lord saying was to be encouraged that Mary and Jesus didn't lose their trust, but they trusted, they were committed, they endured until the end, and God raised them up. This is my hope: that God will raise us up, and we'll be able to see John-Paul again.

"I thought God was done. But during prayer my dear friend Gail Rock, who bears the same cross, came over, put her arm around me, and we went to the cross together and wept together. I feel so tremendously blessed, not only to have a wonderful husband and family and all you sisters, but a special sister in the Lord with whom I share this cross. We can go to the cross together and we can pray for one another. It's a very special gift from the Lord. I want to thank you all, and I thank God and give him the glory for everything he's done."

A friend of ours later told me what was happening in the room as Maureen spoke. "Many women cried," she said. "It was as though God was healing them of the pain they carried for your loss. They were weeping for joy that God had touched Maureen, that he had made one more step of the journey clear to her. The younger women sat stunned. They couldn't even believe she could give herself away like that. But what touched everyone was the miracle of God moving in her heart. We were watching Maureen come through this. It was a rare and privileged moment."

These moments of union with God are often moments of intense joy and pain rolled into one. Some time after Maureen's retreat I was at Eucharistic Adoration. Eucharistic Adoration is a tradition in the Catholic Church dating from the tenth century. Its Biblical basis is found in all four Gospels (in Matthew 26:26, Mark 14:22, and Luke 22:19, Jesus says, ". . . this is my body," and in John 6:51 he says, ". . . the bread that I will give is my flesh for the life of the world"). Catholics and many other Christians believe that the consecrated bread is the actual Body of Christ and not simply a commemoration. From this belief flows the practice of spending time in adoration before the real presence of the Lord. Such adoration has been, for centuries, one of the deepest expressions of prayer in the lives of countless Christians. Jesus present in the tabernacle on the altar is also referred to as the Blessed Sacrament.

As I knelt before the Blessed Sacrament I said, "Lord, I miss him so much." Then I felt a hand on my shoulder. It was that of our dear friend Pat, who lost her husband several years ago. She knew exactly what was going on. She said, "He's very close here." Very close. In the Eucharist, both in Mass and in adoration of the Blessed Sacrament, he is as close as he will ever be until we meet again in heaven. I am one with my son in the Eucharist. I touch him, love him, and speak to him in adoring the Lord with whom he is perfectly one. Heaven and earth touch in Christ. Father and son touch in Christ. I kiss my son in the Eucharist.

I walked outside. Facing the distant landscape, I prayed to God: "Why are you doing this to me? Why is it that when I'm close to you, sorrow and love fill my heart?" And these words immediately came to me: "I'm breaking your heart so you'll know what my heart feels like." In my mind I immediately thought of Simeon's word to Mary: " . . . a sword shall pierce your own soul too" (Luke 2:35 NRSV). In that moment I realized that the two greatest lovers in history both had broken hearts. It was as if God were saying to me, "You can't love as I love until your heart is broken. Only a heart that has been broken by love can love with my love."

Though I am hesitant or even reluctant to admit it, I am coming to believe that God has allowed this separation, as excruciating as it is, to release more love in the world: love flowing down from a young boy immensely powerful in his prayer before the throne of God, and love flowing out to the world from the broken hearts of every member of his family. As the cross is transformed by him who embraced it, I pray that our cross embraced might bring light to those who suffer alone and in darkness.

SIXTEEN

The End of Beginnings

The seasons have their own wordless poetry about death and life. Their constant movement of death and life is mirrored in the Church's cycles of fasting and feasting, Lent and Easter, conversion and new life. We were in midwinter, with its low, flat, gray vistas. Soon the earth would awaken. Crocus and tulip, cherry and dogwood and azalea, will arise from the now-frozen earth to sing their praise of God. Does the sleep analogy used by St. Paul and Jesus finally make sense, revealed in the world of nature? After all, what is more dead than a daffodil under the snow? Nicole will soon be a year old. The "year old" moment signifies in some way the countdown to April 24, the first anniversary of Johnny's death, the last event in the year of firsts.

Despite the glorious rebirth that spring normally signifies, I resented the passage of time. I did not want it to be a year since I was playing with my son. It seemed too far gone. Somehow one month and two months allowed me to think, "He was just here." But a year would be gone and I could not say that. He has not been here for a long time.

Lots of people say the first year is the hardest. Many psychologists say the second year is worse. Beyond the layman and the professional are the saints who can see the bigger picture. They can live joy and sorrow in the same moment. For us, the first year had been a somersault of joys and sorrows. It had been a year filled with intense and proximate reminders, from clothes, to toys, to photographs and memories: a year filled with all the moments in which he was so obviously absent. At the beginning of April, the month of his first anniversary, Maureen and I went out for dinner. She said to me, "I don't know what it is. I've been having a lot more flashbacks. I've been crying a lot more in my prayer time. I want to put more pictures of Johnny up." I looked at her and said, "It's April."

It was April, the month that he died. It was hard to believe that in three short weeks he would be dead a year. A grueling year. At times an unbearable year. Yet as I looked at his smiling face in a photo all I could think was: "Johnny, I'm so glad we had you. I'm so glad for those six-and-one-half years of such delight. In a way I cannot understand and will not understand until eternity, your work was done. I still look at your strong young shoulders and bright blue eyes and think what I would give to have you back, but what a treasure trove of memories you have given us."

Healing comes with the passage of time. The grief eventually falls more gently. In April I was at a conference in midtown Manhattan. During the lunch break, I went into St. Patrick's Cathedral to find the chapel of adoration. As I walked to the back, I passed a pietà. Not as beautiful as Michelangelo's, but a pietà nonetheless. Mary was sitting with Jesus' dead body in such a way that his head was in her lap and his hand in hers. Incredible gesture! Here is a mother with her child asleep on her lap as he had been thousands of times before. But in this moment she is a mother with her dead child in her arms. I cannot look at a pietà without seeing Maureen holding Johnny.

I knelt down before the Blessed Sacrament. It was impossible fully to take in the significance that Christ was here, silent and waiting, eager to receive everything I need to give him. In the heart of Christ there is room for all the sorrow of the world. Enveloped in the silence, I began to pray.

"Lord, I am so grateful to be here—this moment of stillness in the midst of the swirl of activity. So grateful that you're here and that I can speak to you. Grateful that you have saved us and continue to save us. Grateful that this whole sad experience is resolved in you. Thank you for making a home for us, a safe haven, a refuge. You are that home. Your pierced heart is home for all those whose hearts are pierced. You have led me gently, paused when I paused, waited while I spoke, listened to all the anger and pain in my heart. You have listened like no one else could. And I have talked and talked endlessly until my own grief exhausted itself on the shores of your heart. The lower I bent, your face was still beneath me. The higher I gazed, your face was still above me. 'Where can I hide from your spirit? / From your presence, where can I flee?' the psalmist asks (Psalm 139:7). I could turn to you because you are the God who suffers and so I am not alone. You are not just kingly and glorious but poor and scarred." I paused, reflecting on the many turns of the road in this first year. I thought of the amazing, almost miraculous fact that whatever else I struggled with, the absence of God was never an issue. I had never once felt distanced from the Lord. That was the one thing that he would not allow.

"Thank you that you suffered. I could not have walked this path had not the vision of your crucified body been always before me. You have taught me that the road to heaven is paved with suffering as well as joy, that you did not spare even your own Mother the agony of watching your life ebb away. Thank you for redeeming suffering and forging something beautiful out of it." I had come to realize, in the previous few months, that Maureen and I were more deeply in love at the end of this year than we were at its beginning.

"Thank you that you are risen. You bowed down so low that death-darkened earth could not contain you. You bowed down so low that evil could not find a way around you. Your crucified flesh said, 'It stops here.' Evil stops here. Sin stops here. Death stops here. In the face of your victory, evil rolled down the hill of Calvary, your blood closing in on it like the sea upon Pharaoh's charioteers.

"'It is finished,' you said (John 19:30). Yes. It is finished. Death is finished. The separation from God is finished. And your blood, which never ceases to fall upon the earth through the hands of the priest, unleashes again and again a flood tide of mercy.

"Have you answered all my questions? No. Do I need them all answered? No. Would I understand the answers even if you gave them to me? Hardly likely. But you are with me and you have been the light in my darkness. Even as I struggled with what you allowed to happen, I have known within my heart the constant refrain: 'Lord, to whom would we go?'

"The road I've been walking I have not walked alone. You are total openness, total receptivity, a presence and unconditional love that I cannot begin to comprehend. In sharing everything with you—the crying out in the night, the not understanding, the desolation—it is here that I have found rest for my soul. You have bent down and drawn me to yourself. You could not have loved me more."

I knelt down and kissed the cold stone floor of the chapel, so blessed to be near the altar that held the Lord. I returned to the conference, but I have no idea what transpired that afternoon. My mind never left the chapel. I had found rest for my soul. At the end of the day, that was what I wanted more than anything else. Not the rest of sleep to find temporary respite from the pain, but rest in the Lord—the sure knowledge that after I have ranted and raved, railed and wept, said everything I can think of about how much I hate that this has happened, I am understood, accepted, and loved. That was true rest for my soul.

As the year moved on toward Johnny's first anniversary, the harsh, dull winter yielded to the color and fragrance of spring, and the penitence of Lent yielded to the glory of Easter. Easter was complicated in that year of firsts. It was a day and a season of both joy and sorrow. The complication of Easter was not on the level of the intellect but of the emotions. I could only think back to last Easter and prior Easters. Last Easter, John-Paul was Nicole's proud big brother.

Last Easter we were walking up and down the street together at the Easter parade. Last Easter he looked so boyish, so handsome, so confident, so in love with everything and everyone that came his way. My deepest experience of Easter this year was gratitude. It was not an emotional experience. I did not "feel" grateful the way one "feels" happy. I *was* grateful. Grateful for the sacrifice of Christ. Grateful for his obedience to the Father's will. Grateful for his resurrection, the assurance of eternal life to all who follow him. Last Easter we laughed and ate candy and wrestled and played "get on the floor and catch me." This Easter was a longing for him and a longing for Christ and the severe grace of knowing that all shall be well and that he is safe in the hands of the Lord.

The year moved inexorably to our last first: the anniversary of Johnny's death. The days leading up to it were filled with flashbacks. Johnny on the lawn. Johnny on the stretcher. Johnny not breathing. Johnny in the ambulance, the hospital, the casket, the ground. The scenes appeared like so many frames in a movie.

On April 24, his anniversary, I took the day off work. I had decided that I would make it a retreat day. In the morning we went as a family to plant flowers at his grave. We took turns speaking quietly to him. Then we all went out for breakfast. It was a day fraught with memories. At 3:20 P.M. I walked to the place where he was hit. I knelt down and prayed and wept at the place where I found him and David. As the afternoon unfolded, friends began to stop by as they had on Johnny's birthday, with flowers, notes, and treats for the children. In the evening our pastor came over and offered Mass in our home. Johnny's cousins, aunts, uncles, and grandparents, as well as our closest friends, were there. Once again we gathered at the table of the Lord where heaven and earth embrace, where Christ himself comes to console and strengthen, to gladden hearts, to lift burdens, to give strength.

Time is a healer. It does not heal everything but it does heal some things: A year had gone by and I do not think we were trusting God any more than in the early months, but we were freer of the weight of it all. The healing of grief takes time. It takes much more than time, but it does take time. One should be very wary of other people's time lines for one's grief; after all, the loss is not theirs. Grief is a journey. How long it takes is wrapped up in the mystery of the unique person who is grieving. So many factors enter into this equation: age, health, family background, culture, faith perspective, closeness, to name a few. The prescription for healing will be different for each one.

The Jews have a phrase that encapsulates their grieving process: "a week, a month, a year." For me, the first year was one of intense grief. But as Johnny's first anniversary approached, I was ready for a change in the way I related to this chapter of our lives.

I could never forget him. I carry him in my heart, everywhere. But the pain does lessen. It had better lessen: The soul cannot live in endless agony—it would cave in. I can often talk to him and about him without pain, but not always. I suspect the other moments, the ones that reduce Maureen and me to silence or to tears, will be there until we die. But there is peace. God heals the brokenhearted.

For months I had thought my heart would never be healed. I did not even want it to be. But glimmers of light and hope did reappear, sure as the morning sun on the water. Christ has died. Christ is risen. Christ will come again. At the end of the year of firsts I realized that God had been at work in my heart, knitting together all the frayed edges. He had done the same for Maureen and the children. He was not filling the void. No, the void is there like a mathematical equation. Subtract one from any number and there is always less. It was the pain that had begun to disappear, and the joy that was coming back into focus. We came to the realization that we yield our grief in different ways, at different times—and the realization that we can trust God to bring to completion what he has begun.

SEVENTEEN

Grace to Press On

The psychological perspective that the second year is harder stems from the fact that the shock and numbness have worn off to some degree. One thing I can say with certainty about the year of firsts: There was no way around it. The only way out was through. The first year was often better, and often worse, than either of us could have predicted. A year later Nicole was not an infant and Maureen was not so exhausted. A year later Maureen began to feel things she had not been able to feel or had not allowed herself to feel. A year later there were many things for her to deal with, things that she simply had not had the time or energy to process in the aftermath of the accident while caring for a new baby. For Maureen, perspective would come later. Maureen is more private and reserved than I am. We respect these differences in our relationship. As Maureen helped me through the first year by her strength and stability, it was now my turn to help her through the second year by eliciting what was going on inside her and walking with her as she moved through it.

As time moved on we saw changes in our relationship with Johnny. And while the second year was in many ways harder than the first for Maureen, it also brought the time when we could speak of Johnny without pain. It heralded the time when we could speak of him and feel joy in our hearts. It did not take an entire year for this to happen. There had always been moments when we spoke of Johnny with joy. But it was joy that was a break from the pain, joy that was an interruption, joy that was a splash of bright color on the dull palette of grief. By the second year, at least for me, it became joy tinged with wistfulness, joy tinged with loneliness, joy bordered by an edge of longing—but mainly joy. I knew the rest would come for Maureen.

Two months after the first anniversary of Johnny's death, the older children each wrote to him. I encouraged them to do this at the suggestion of a friend of mine who works with dying children and their families. We were eager to hear what they would have to say, so I asked them if Maureen and I could read their letters. Gregory was eleven; Thérèse, ten; and David, eight.

July 1, '96

Dear Johnny,

What is it like to enter the narrow gate and hear God say "well done, good and faithful servant"? To lay your head on Mary's shoulder or fight side-by-side with Saint Michael the Archangel in the raging battle between good and evil. Johnny, I'm sure these are just a few of the many things you do in heaven. You must pray for us a lot because when we pray to you our prayers are usually answered in a short period of time.

I really miss you a lot. When I think of you (more often than not) tears fill my eyes, as I remember the great times we shared together. I think your death had a great impact on many people's lives. I know it had one on mine. I think your death has drawn me closer to the Lord, and through your intercession I have been able to pray at Mass in a whole new way.

And so I ask you, Johnny, please continue to pray for our family so that we may reach our only goal in life, heaven, where we will be greeted by your smiling face.

With great love,

Greg

6/30/96

Dear Johnny,

I love you so, so, so very much.

I miss you so much. And what I really, really miss is your smile and your laughter and your sense of humor and everything about you. You were the sweetest and nicest little boy and brother. No one could replace you even if they tried their hardest.

You are the best little brother anybody could have. I love you so much. This has been very hard for me and everyone but, you and God, Mom and Dad, the kids and friends got me and everyone through it. Especially you and God and Mary. I love you very much and I miss you very much but I know that I will see you again and you will see me.

Love, your big sister,

Thérèse Eileen

P.S. Please pray for me every day and even though you don't need prayers I will pray for you every day! I love you!

Date: 6/30/96

Dear J.P.,

How's it up in heaven? I really miss you. I wish you were here. I've been so lonely without you. There's no one to play with if Mike can't play. The house has been so different without you. I wish you weren't gone. Life would be so much happier if you were here. I love you so very much. You're the best. I love you.

Love, David

173

We had made the decision to let them be how and who they were and not force them into a molded response. We kept making time for them to talk about Johnny, to laugh, cry, commemorate, remember. We spoke about our pain to signal that it was okay for them to feel pain. We tried to balance real human suffering with real Christian hope. And we prayed.

We used the talking cure. We encouraged them to talk out what was going on inside them. When we talk about fear, we begin to exorcise fear. The same goes with pain, sadness, anger, grief. None of these is bad in itself. But when we do not "talk them out" we virtually promise ourselves sickness later in life.

A few days after reading their letters, Maureen and I were having coffee in the living room. David and Gregory were in the kitchen washing dishes. David said to Gregory, "Do you have an age when you think you're going to die? How old do you think you're going to be when you die?" *Marked:* The children are marked by the death of their brother. Marked just as David's left shin is marked, where the bike chain cut into his leg upon impact with the car. They still talk very freely about Johnny, though less frequently. Life is full of school, friends, sports, music, celebrations. They are happy and affectionate. And they are marked. The scar on David's leg does not hurt anymore. But when they ask a question like that one, I realize how deeply they are affected.

I said to Maureen, "A nine-year-old boy wouldn't ask that question in the normal course of events. Most nine-year-olds and eleven-year-olds aren't touched by death so closely." I am grateful they speak about it. When they bring it out, we can work with it. When it is hidden and repressed, then we have a problem.

Rose was five and in kindergarten. When Johnny died she was four, and a lot seemed to pass her by. But as time unfolds she has said some extraordinarily perceptive things. We first noticed it at the cemetery. We would go every few weeks to visit. While the other kids would start to wander, Rosie would stand near the grave and quietly talk to John-Paul. When I asked her about it, she would say, "I'm just talking to him." This child knows something special. Once she was at the kitchen table, drawing. She drew four people. "Who are they?" I asked. "Jesus, me, Johnny, and the Blessed Mother." Sixteen months had passed and she still drew him into her pictures. It was her way of drawing him into her heart, her way of remembering, accepting, processing. At dinner Susanna, now three, told me she was a woman. I said to her jokingly, "You're not a woman, you're a girl!" "No, I'm a woman!" she retorted. "No," I said, "you'll be a woman when you're 32." Rose then said, "How do you know she'll make it to 32? She may die before then." Once again, evidence that a once safe world had been shaken loose from its secure moorings. Rose knows someone who did not make it to 32.

Rose asked me several times during the early months of the second year if I would take her to "see Johnny." The first time she asked I responded, "You can't go see Johnny. He's in heaven." She responded with the two-syllable "Da-ad" that kids say when they have had it with the silliness of their parents. I smiled and so did she. "No, Dad, I mean a visit to his grave." "Why do you want to visit Johnny's grave?" I asked. "I like to," she replied. "It reminds me of him." "And what do you think of when you think of him?" "How much I love him and how much I miss him."

The following Saturday I had a lunch-time errand. Rose got in the car and we went to the cemetery. She loves that special time with Maureen or me. When we got to Johnny's grave, I asked her, "What does the stone say?" "I will see you again and your hearts will be full of joy." "Why don't we both say something to Johnny?" "Johnny, I love you and I miss you." "Yeah, Johnny, so do I," I said, "but I'm so glad you're in heaven." Then we left.

As we drove along, she continued to talk. "Johnny and I used to play together every day when the other kids were at school. What's hard now is when Mommy puts Susanna and Nicole in for naps I don't have anyone to play with." A moment's pause. "Dad, one day I'm going to get married and on my wedding day I'm going to come here. And then one day I'm going to have children. And I'm going to bring them here. And when they say, 'Who's that?' I'm going to say, 'That's my brother.'"

What about Susanna and Nicole? They were so young. Maureen said once, "They'll have all the joy of knowing they have a brother in heaven without all the pain of losing him on earth." This is true. I suspect, however, that his death will impact them, too, in terms of loss: "I have a brother I never knew." That is a hole. One day you will know him, dear sweet girls; when death will be destroyed he will charge gloriously and golden into your lives. For now, though, there are memories and hope. Memories we can feed you with, pictures to hang on the walls of your soul, of the innumerable charming, boyish things he did with each of you. Even you, Nicole. His hand prints and kisses are all over you, and his laughter is deep in your ear.

Our eighth child, Catherine Elise, was born two years after Johnny died. Katie, as we call her, was like the sunlight that came after the storm. I held her one night shortly after she was born and we walked past Johnny's picture. And I said to her, "Katie, you will never know him. I'm so sorry you will never know him." But this is not absolutely correct. You will see him. You will meet him. Such is Christ's victory that you will know him in a way that will make you feel as though you had never been without him, when time yields to eternity, and he ushers you into the presence of the Lord.

The children are happy, lively, high-energy kids for the most part. They also have a kind of knowledge that most children their age do not possess. It comes out in countless unpremeditated comments about life and death, tragedy and suffering, God and heaven. Even though their grief is largely healed, it still visits them from time to time as an unexpected guest.

David, for instance, had to write about a saint in school. Whom did he choose?

Saint David Floyd

David loved God very much. He was one of ten children. In 1995, he and his brother were hit. David was injured but his brother died. We were very sad. They forgave the person who did it. We still miss him very much. But then his parents died. God told David to become a priest. So he did. He became a priest for three years. He was a priest and then he died as a martyr. He had his head chopped off.

Ten children: He included his mother's three miscarriages in the family roster (Katie had not yet arrived on the scene). He talked about the death of his parents. He talked about being a martyr and having his head chopped off. The background to the dark cross he colored was blood red. This child was dealing with death. He was very aware of it. At the same time, he was very open with me. We talked regularly about many things: hamsters, his relationship with his brothers and sisters, his temper, his friends, school, and John-Paul. Eighteen months after Johnny died, we went out to breakfast for my monthly check-up with him.

"Do you miss him?" I asked. "Yeah. I miss him." "How much?" "A lot." "How often do you think about him?" "Every day." "How do you feel when you think about him?" "Sad." Sad. "Do you ever cry when you think about him?" "Sometimes at night when I'm in my bed I think about him and I cry. Not all the time. Sometimes." "And you know it's okay to cry, right?" "Yeah. You gotta get it out. Because if you don't get it out when you're a kid, you have big problems later on." "That's right, son. You've got to keep letting it out. The sadness is easing, but you need to let it out when it comes."

Eighteen months since Johnny had died, and David still thought about him every day. As a family, we were laughing, playing, working, and praying. But at that point we laughed, played, worked, and prayed with a hole in our hearts. What another mother who lost a son told us is true: "It's like chronic back pain—you learn to live with it."

In the second year, going to visit Johnny's grave was no longer just pain, however cathartic and necessary that pain was. No, visiting the grave became a place of encounter, a sacred place. I would still say to him, "Johnny, I wish this hadn't happened and I wish you were here," but it was not a denial of faith or of the power and love of God. I am not sure he wants it different than it is. There is a void. The hurt and the hole are a continuous reminder that I am not whole because I am not home. It is important for me to remember I am not home: otherwise I make here-and-now into an idol. Having part of my here-and-now gone cautions me against such foolishness. The very loneliness is a grace. It is the recognition that I am created for more.

One thing for sure: God does not remove the broken heart all at once and give a new, happy one. I had to be wary of looking for a quick fix. Besides, there is too much he wants to teach me. The healing of the brokenhearted is the ability to acknowledge pain and loss and to trust God in spite of them. Christ, through the grace of the Holy Spirit, was knitting my heart back together. He would go down so deep I could not even feel what he was doing. But he was busy. He went down deeper than the pain. His love is always bigger than pain, though the more we love, the more we suffer. That is the price of love. And although we have paid a price because we have loved, countless others have filled our coffers with the wealth of their own sympathy and kindness. One particular story comes to mind.

On the second anniversary of Johnny's death, David had a Cub Scout weekend overnight. I did not want to go, but David asked and I knew he needed this special fun time with his friends and me. Saturday night brought a special gift. After we put the kids in their tents, Gary and I talked a long time by the fire.

Gary Montemurno is one of my dearest friends. He can do anything with cars and tools. Beyond what he can do, however, Gary is like a canvas that God himself is stretching. Gary once thought of himself as a mechanic; now he is the president of a company. Part of this change was a matter of Gary discovering who he is; part of it was other men revealing him to himself. A huge part of it was his wife, Alicia, loving him into the man that he is today. I told him once: "You have one picture of who you are. God has a different one. Take your pick. You can either go with the limited version bound by sin, shame, disappointment, and past history, or you can go with the unconditionally loved and accepted and unique one that God has in mind." Gary has surmounted much, with the grace of God.

Surmounted, but not forgotten. The person one meets, therefore, is an impressive, articulate, confident, take-charge man, who is at the same time one of the most approachable men one could ever hope to meet. He reminds me of the line about the sinful woman: "So I tell you, her many sins have been forgiven; hence, she has shown great love. But the one to whom little is forgiven, loves little" (Luke 7:47). Gary has always shown me great love. So it was no surprise, in retrospect, that I would have ended up spending the weekend of Johnny's second anniversary on a Cub Scout overnight with him and our boys. When we finally got the boys to bed, we sat a long while before the fire.

"How are you doing, two years out?" he asked. "Not a fair question on the weekend of his second anniversary!" I responded. "At the moment, more sorrow than joy; more absence than presence. The week of the anniversary is a flood of memories, some having to do with sheer delight of Johnny, most having to do with the accident, the hospital, the images that are no less graphic two years out.

"Gary, I know all the theological facts. But there are other facts as well. It is hard living without him. An anniversary brings into vivid relief the colors that begin to exist in a softer hue. The pain has diminished. The raw nerves have become a dull ache, and the dull ache isn't felt all the time. I can savor memories, and they don't cause me pain in the savoring." Then he looked at me as the fire glowed before us and we felt its warmth on our hands and faces. "We carry your pain in our hearts," he said.

"Gary," I said, "anyone who has experienced the death of a child desperately wants to talk about it. There are many things bereaved parents want to share. But we dread foisting it upon someone. Therefore, we can't really talk until someone invites us, until someone really wants to know. In a certain sense we can only be rescued by the hand of another. You have done this for me on a weekend I didn't even want to be on. Thank you. Thank you for carrying the pain. Thank you for saying it, two years later."

Grief and time. Grief and memory. Grief and the seasons of growth. Like hailstones in a summer storm, I know these moments will be with the children and with us until we die. Are we stuck in them? By no means. But they are part of us. We are parents who have lost a child. They are brothers and sisters who have lost a brother. It is a defining moment for them. It is not the only moment. But it is one that is with us until memory is lost in the ever-present Now of heaven.

I read from Matthew's Gospel: "Come to me, all you who labor and are burdened, and I will give you rest. Take my yoke upon you and learn from me, for I am meek and humble of heart; and you will find rest for yourselves. For my yoke is easy and my burden light" (Matthew 11:28-30). If I accept the invitation to come to Christ, I will find refreshment. The refreshment is mainly interior. Two years later I can say, "Christ has refreshed my soul." The refreshment is not constant. It is sometimes in the realm of emotions and sometimes not. But it is deeper than emotion. Christ is a miner searching the crevices of my soul. He descends to the absolute depths and finds what is raw, hurting, or damaged, and puts the pieces back together, sometimes with a kiss and sometimes with the chisel of his grace.

After the first few months I did not think of Johnny every hour. After two years I still think of him every day. I cannot yet imagine going a day without thinking about him. We are enjoying our life as a couple and a family. The immanent life force which is Christ himself keeps on bursting through. The confident hope of seeing Johnny again is like the air we breathe.

And the words of God ring truer than my emotions. I love going to his grave because the juxtaposition of the body of death and the word of life is so fierce. I go because while my heart still experiences moments of sorrow and pain, it also experiences soaring hope. "I will see you again and your hearts will be full of joy." The word of God stands forever. Death does not stand forever. Death is swallowed up in the victory of eternal life. And while for the moment love and suffering are entwined, the day will come when love will swallow up suffering ever more surely than the earth swallowed the body of John-Paul.

There are two icons that express this season of our lives: the broken body of Christ on the cross and the broken body of John-Paul on our front lawn. Christ on the cross. I realize I have spent two years looking at his body, bruised and broken, hanging on a cross. And I realize anew: Christ suffered. We worship a God who suffers: Christ who died and the Father who suffered the Passion of his Son. We worship a God who felt terror, abandonment, bewilderment, loneliness, and the misunderstanding of even his closest friends. In Christ we have somewhere to go when these feelings belong to us. If God had not suffered, the world would go mad. The world is mad at this very moment, and it is mad for precisely this reason: It has not accepted its own suffering and connected it to his. We are all going to suffer. When we make the connection between his suffering and ours, redemption comes.

Christ took all the sin of the world upon his shoulders and let it crush him. Utterly. And after the most profound "yes" that was ever offered, the Father gave life back to him and made him Lord. This is what is compelling about the cross: its two aspects of suffering and glory. Christ suffered in the extreme for us, and by his suffering he assured that two things will happen to our suffering: First, it will have meaning when linked through prayer to the cross. Second, it will be over. A better day is coming: new heavens and a new earth, new bodies, unbent, unbroken, unstained by tears. This is our hope. We are not meant for death and sorrow but for life and joy.

EIGHTEEN

The Strength of Surrender

Two years of working my way through grief and the intellectual struggles that accompany the most dramatic questions of love have led me to a new moment of surrender. Surrender implies commitment, but it is 99 percent the work of grace. I cannot force myself to surrender. I yield to it, like a sexual embrace. Once it builds, there is an inevitability to it. Even if I put it off for as long as I can, I still desire its fulfillment. For me, this surrender is the continual letting go of Johnny and my attachment to him. It is at the same time a cleaving to the will of God, allowing him full sway in my life, with no hidden pockets of resentment.

God's dominion extends to the death of our son. The real evil that happened, he can handle. That is the good theology I learned in school. But there is more to life than good theology. In the crucible of suffering, Maureen and I learned a way of speaking to God and relating to God beyond anything we had previously experienced. In our suffering, God was with us in a dimension of intimacy beyond anything we could have imagined. God has led us through grief to a new place. His dominion does not mean that he wills everything, but that even when tragic and evil things happen, he is still God. And if God, then Love.

I have also learned that the theology of hope and the psychology of grief are two different things. They are autonomous realities. Each needs to be given its proper place. Hope is an expectation that needs and desires will be fulfilled. Its object is not in the present, but the future. The theology of hope assures us that we will see Johnny again, that he is happy beyond description, that he is watching over us and praying for us.

The problem is that often people think the theological reasons for hope displace the psychological reasons for grief. They do not. When a child dies (I am sure this is true of many other deaths, but I can only speak of this one), one grieves. One experiences heaviness, pressure, desolation, loneliness, sadness, disruption in patterns of eating, sleeping, and relating. One is exhausted emotionally and physically. This does not mean one has no hope; it simply means one has an abundance of grief.

I learned that I must honor grief by giving it its time. Grieving takes time, and nothing speeds up the process, not even hope. Why? Because they are two different realities. I cannot press on the horn to make the car go faster: The horn and the accelerator involve two essentially different mechanisms, however united they are in the body of the car. The same is true of grief and hope.

We experienced the presence of God along every step of the journey of grief. But he was with us in the pain, not lifting us out of the pain. He was walking the tortuous route with us, not paving a straight path. He waited with us when we had to pause, not pushing us to a premature resolution of a problem that has no quick fix. More than lifting our grief, I believe that God invited us to offer it to him. He wanted us to be actively involved in our healing. He knew we could not give him more than a bit at a time because we did not want to. The healing happened very slowly. We remembered, we accepted, we allowed ourselves to feel it all, and we laid it at the foot of the cross when the grace came to do that.

Gradually and almost imperceptibly, the joyful thoughts of Johnny became more prominent than the sorrowful ones. When I think of Johnny now, I do not see a dead child on my front lawn. I see radiant beauty. I see life, joy, and love. And while I wait for our family to be reunited, I wait with him in the Eucharist. The Eucharist is like a laser that cuts through the veil that separates us from those we love. Call the veil time, call it death. It still separates, and that separation is painful. But in receiving the Body and Blood of the Lord, I am one with those who have gone on before me. The more faithfully and reverently I receive the Eucharist, the more real heaven becomes. The veil gets thinner, until one day it shall disappear.

While I await that day I move back and forth in time, in memory and hope. For so many months after Johnny's death Maureen and I kept having flashbacks. But I am also experiencing "flash forwards." They are like the lines of a poem I read many years ago:

> . . . while slicing a fried egg,
> while opening a gate
> were two of the times . . .
> a high, unattended sixteenth note
> calling what seemed his name.

Our experiences are like that: a tiny window opening for just a moment onto reality. And what is reality? This is what I began to pray:

"You are perfectly trustworthy and you know what you are doing. You are sovereign and all-loving in Johnny's death and its impact on us. You are using it to draw us more deeply to yourself. We are being drawn. You are the Lord of the void as well as the Lord of the fullness, Lord of the desolation as well as the consolation. The children are marked, but they love you. They hurt, but they believe in you. They have moments of grief, but they trust you. You hold us in your hands. You have held us in your hands the whole way through. We are held and we are carried. Is it possible that your attention could be so personal and so particular?" These windows open just long enough for me to whisper in the dark, "I trust you."

"Yes, you are in charge. You gave us enough faith that we were not devastated by our loss. You knew the pain would be good for us. You knew Johnny wanted to be with you more than he wanted to be with us. You knew we would be better for our brief time with him, and what's more, you knew he would be better for his brief time with us. Your will was that he was here and your will is that he is there. And your will is that we live with a void—sometimes a gentle ache like a child's momentary cry in the middle of the night, sometimes a yawning chasm that nothing seems to fill.

"Yes, you heal the brokenhearted. But not in the way people think. You heal us to the point of recognizing that we will never be whole until we are home with you. It makes the images you give us for life so much more real—a battle, a journey, a narrow road. Through it all, your love carries us and works it to the good."

"Are you and Maureen ever going to be the same?" The question was not asked with any impatience or aggravation. An interesting question, nonetheless, coming from J.J. He had said earlier in our conversation, "It has been hard for your friends. It's been hard watching you and Maureen suffer. It's been hard seeing you in so much pain. It's been frustrating not knowing what to do or how to help. I know you've said just being there was a help, but it's been hard being able to do nothing more than just be there."

I am sure this is true. It is hard to be with someone in intense pain and not be able to take the pain away. But God never makes universal and absolute promises to take pain away, other than in the eschatological fulfillment of history in heaven. Jesus suffered the agony in the garden. Did God take the pain away? No. We do not pray "The Consolation in the Garden," we pray "The Agony in the Garden." But God did send an angel, a spirit who ministered his presence and his love.

Good friends are like angels. Our friends brought us God's presence and love. They did not solve our problems, as if grief were a problem to be solved. They did not dispense pious phrases. Our closest friends allowed us to be in as much pain as we were in and did not trivialize it by trying to move us beyond it. The angel in the garden did not say to Jesus, "There, there." In fact, we do not know what the angel said, or if the angel said anything at all. We are quite uncomfortable with not having anything to say.

The answer to J.J.'s question is simple. No, we are never going to be the same. There is no turning back, no becoming again what we were before Johnny died. The school of suffering has taught us lessons that can be learned only in its hallways. We are different.

Love anything and your heart will break, as C.S. Lewis has said. We gave our heart to this boy as completely as we could and he took off with it. I realize that sometimes the reason I feel so strange is that part of my heart is not here any more. I gave it to Johnny and he took it with him. I often am struck with wonder at the thought of that gleeful little imp running away with my heart, hiding it in heaven like some divine version of hide-and-seek. As a consequence, Maureen and I find ourselves caring less about a whole host of concerns, because Johnny's death has made our longing for heaven grow exponentially.

For the last few summers we have gone back to Long Beach Island. We unpack and then go for a walk along the beach. I do not know if I will ever go to a beach again without seeing Johnny. Johnny loved the beach. Now, walking the beach with Maureen and the children is joyful and painful at the same time. The pain still sneaks up on us. It is still hard not to have him with us. Family moments still never seem quite complete; family photos are always unfinished. But with grace and the passage of time each vacation has been better than the one before it. The first year, with Johnny dead only six weeks, we were reeling from the blow. But each successive year has brought us to a place of greater peace, for which we can only thank God. And memory will, I am confident, continue to hold out to us more blessing and less pain and sorrow.

Things will never be "back to normal." Life will be full of peace and joy, love and sorrow, sin and reconciliation, but not "back to normal." We have a new norm for normal. Reality has changed, the psychological and spiritual terrain has changed. We are possessed of a terrible wisdom about life that we did not have before. Like Jacob wrestling with the angel, part of us is knocked out of joint, and we see differently, feel differently, know differently.

The worst nightmare to a parent has happened. Our child is dead. And God has proved true to his word: He has healed, is healing, and will continue to heal us. Now we know more. We know both the healing and the brokenness, and we know that God is unfailingly with us and for us.

For six-and-a-half years we were blessed with a very special gift. We are still blessed. Even in his death, Johnny has brought us gifts. Our family has grown closer through this experience. We have seen as never before the treasure that our friends are to us. Suffering has opened our eyes to the many sufferings of those around us and given us the understanding and desire to help them. It has given us access to God in a way we never thought possible.

And so I live with the loss. I do not deny it. It is there, sometimes felt and sometimes unfelt, sometimes raging and sometimes still. I am alive not in spite of this loss but with this loss. I can laugh, sing, dance, with a hole in my heart. I can even praise. This is the grace of healing. It does not diminish Johnny in any way. On the contrary, he is honored when the rest of us go after God and the life we have been given with every bit as much joy and abandon as he did, knowing that nothing can separate the love we share, not even death. It is only upward from here, my sunshine boy, until I see your smiling face.

~Fifteen Years Later~

NINETEEN

These Things Remain

Fifteen years after Johnny died, and eleven years after the publication of *A Grief Unveiled*, a call came from the editor of Paraclete Press. "We want to bring your book out again, but we want to know what happened next." It's hard to think about what happened next when "next" involves fifteen years and ten people's lives, including the birth of two children who weren't here when Johnny died. That's a lot of next. Kids who were not yet teens are in their mid-twenties and the two who were not yet born are twelve and fourteen. Gregory is pursuing a PhD in philosophy. Therese is a pediatric oncology nurse. David is recently married and teaching at an inner-city school in Houston. Rose and Susanna, who can barely remember Johnny, are in college. Nicole is a junior in high school, and Katie is a freshman. Maria, the youngest, is twelve and in sixth grade, and is no longer the baby.

It is difficult to point to one image or an experience that would bring together the normalcy as well as the poignancy of these intervening fifteen years. But after the publisher called, I started looking for an "entry ramp," something I could climb onto in order to get the story moving. It came at a moment I didn't expect.

July 30, 2011.

"Good evening, everyone. It is my honor and great pleasure tonight to say a few words to our bride and groom. To my brother and sister-in-law. I have known Dave for, well, his entire life, and would like to begin by saying, 'Dave, you married up.' But, as the women in my life often remind me, *every man marries up!*" This was our eldest, Gregory, speaking at his brother's wedding.

"And Kara, let me tell you from decades of personal experience, he's a great roommate. I'm sure you'll complement one another perfectly: you're neat, well-dressed, hygienic . . . and Dave is none of those things.

"I remember when Dave called me up the fall of his senior year to tell me he was thinking about asking out this girl he'd met. I, of course, thought this was great. (I also assumed that when Dave got a girlfriend everyone would stop bothering me about getting one. I was wrong—it only gets worse.) Anyway, I asked where they'd met, expecting something along the lines of a party, a school event, in a class even. But no, where did Dave meet Kara? The LIBRARY: they met in the library! WHO meets in the library? Does it get any nerdier?

"Dave met his future wife in the least romantic space on a college campus, indeed, perhaps in the entire world—you're not even allowed to talk! This is the stuff Disney movies are made of, right? Wrong. But oh, it gets better. . . .

"The other side of the story, I learned recently, was that, having met Dave, Kara made sure to study *in the exact same spot* for the next few weeks so he'd know where to find her.

"They reached their first major milestone when, after the requisite Facebook stalking and instant message-flirting, they finally broke the verbal communication barrier—much to the chagrin of the Holy Cross librarians.

"Kara's name began popping up more regularly in Floyd family conversation, but we still had no in-person sighting. Dave wouldn't tell us her last name in an ultimately vain attempt to prevent some good-natured sibling reconnaissance. However, not easily dissuaded, my sister Rose and I traveled out to visit Dave hoping to spot her across the quad. He refused to let us meet her. We became suspicious. Maybe there was something wrong with her? Maybe he hadn't told her he came from a family the size of a small South American tribe? Maybe she wasn't REAL?!

"But sure enough, with a little more time Kara began appearing at family gatherings, and it wasn't long before she had snuck her way into our hearts—I'll warn you, she's small and quick. Gradually we began to realize that this beautiful young woman, despite all her *summa cum laude* smarts, actually *wanted* to date *Dave*. Initially, we thought maybe she had lost a bet.

"Now, despite their, shall we say, "auspicious" beginning in the Holy Cross library, a major hurdle lay ahead. You see Dave and Kara come from different, and indeed at times opposed, religious backgrounds. I'm not referring to where they worship on Sunday morning. I'm referring to who they root for on Saturday afternoon! Kara is from Boston and Dave from New Jersey, and, as we all know, there are no teams in Connecticut worth compromising on.

"But, true love conquering all, Dave and Kara have agreed on a 'Sporting Prenuptial Agreement' to raise their children in the 'faith,' which is to say, cheering for New York-Area sports teams and the Fighting Irish of Notre Dame (at least this is what I'm told).

"On a more serious note, though, however divergent their sports affinities, what Dave and Kara are in absolute agreement on and what suits you two so well for one another and what has endeared you so much to all of us is your love for each other, for your faith, and for other people.

"Before meeting one another each of you had made the decision to put other people's lives ahead of your own. Between the two of you you've spent time in Mexico, Kenya, and Nicaragua, not to mention your time spent in the United States serving the victims of natural disaster, the mentally and physically disabled, and the underprivileged students you now teach in Houston. This is truly remarkable. You've put service toward others at the center of your lives, and it has spilled over into your relationship with one another.

"And this is something that we've all experienced from you. If you'll permit me to wax philosophical for just the briefest moment, I would add that when you enter into a relationship with someone, that relationship becomes a *space*; it becomes a *place* that other people can enter into. You have both been a place where we can come; a place we can enter into to be loved and appreciated; to be reminded of who we are. A haven full of life and joy.

"Kara, as I'm sure you've come to see, Dave is a passionate and loyal person. And I can promise you that he's made his choice. He will love you and be faithful to you from this life into the next.

"David, you're my brother, and I love you. And I've learned from you what it means to love a woman. I have no doubt you will be as tremendous a husband and a father as you have been a brother and a friend.

"I would be remiss if I did not close by acknowledging the fact that I am speaking on behalf of two best men tonight; and that the wedding party—sizeable as it is—is still one groomsman short today. Dave, I know that if Johnny were here as you and I are able to be here he would give you and Kara his characteristic 'fist pull' and drawn out 'yessss!' But I also know that he is here in a different way, residing in the hearts and riding on the laughter of so many of us who know and love him. I don't think I can do any better than to pray that the light and joy and laughter that characterized his too-short life with us would be reborn throughout your life with Kara. I spent some time with him preparing this toast, and I know he is very happy that today, in a very special way, and for the first time in a long time, you have a new best friend.

"I'd ask everyone to raise their glasses to Dave and Kara, our dear friends whose marriage holds much hope for us, for the Church, and for the world. May God bless you both with joy and happiness, a long and abundant life filled with His grace and blessing. May you be surrounded by family and friends who multiply your joys and share your sorrows. And may you always be aware of the presence and love of a God who has destined you for one another from eternity, who loves you beyond all measure and who calls you to Himself. To Dave and Kara!"

Maureen and I looked at each other as if to ask: "Did you know he was going to do that?" The boy who was eleven when Johnny died is now twenty-seven and had no need to discuss with his parents what he was going to say at his brother's wedding. We were taken by surprise, but it was a surprise of the best kind. His words were poignant without being distracting or sad. The moment was real, more real than not having said it would have been. Hearing him speak, I knew I had found my entry ramp. Why?

Because it encapsulated the hard-won reality that in Christ, life triumphs over death and love triumphs over loss. Gregory's toast was a highlight in an extended moment—the whole wedding day—that saw David looking happier than we had seen him since Johnny died. It was a perch from which I could look back to view the terrain of the past fifteen years, a place of love and truth and joy. It was a good lens through which to view the passage of so much time.

David was happy—almost incredibly so. David was whole. The child whom we worried about in the aftermath of the accident—would he be okay, would he have survivor guilt, would he have a good life—had grown up, finished high school, studied abroad, graduated from Holy Cross, and met the girl he'd been hoping and praying for and was deeply in love with her. He had just finished two years with Teach for America, was finishing his master's degree in education while teaching at an inner-city all-boys public school in Houston, and was passionate about leveling the educational playing field for disadvantaged children. He was living a life of faith, even if he had unresolved questions about why the Lord had allowed all this to happen to him and his brother and his family.

He had sat in our hotel room in Providence, Rhode Island, earlier that morning. Just the three of us. He started to speak, and then his eyes filled up with tears. That same sensitive nature he had had as a boy had not disappeared: it had only grown richer as it had become woven through a confident and effortlessly masculine nature, complex and uncomplicated at the same time. "I'm really happy," he said, his voice breaking. And he was. There was so much in that moment: so much love, so much history, so much memory and for us, so much relief. It was a priceless gift to Maureen and me as we embraced him and prayed with him. There were no festering psychological wounds, no huge anger issues, no long-term traumatic residue. Even the troublesome and seemingly unanswerable questions of the "why would God allow this?" sort were able to be put somewhere else so that he could love this moment of his wedding day and the gift of Kara, his bride.

It has been fifteen years since Johnny died. After that amount of time, things have had a chance to sift and settle. There have been so many incidents, memories, points of view, temptations, ideas; so many tentative conclusions about what gets held onto and what gets released. There have been resolute rejections (God did not cause the accident) and soft acceptances (God allowed the accident to happen and that is complicated). Like the tides and storms that change the contour of the beach, some things go and some things stay. The things that remain came from many places, some expected and some, surprising. After all these years, what has remained?

1. SPIRITUAL LIFE. I would say that faith made, and continues to make, all the difference. God has been our help and we have never felt abandoned by Him. He was present at the beginning and He has remained present ever since. He is a trustworthy and loving Father who is not unmoved by the suffering of His children. He drew near to us then, and continues to draw near to us now. Sometimes it took a particular event to reveal just how much has happened on the level of healing from Johnny's death. On the fourteenth anniversary of his death, one such event happened that corresponded with the thirty-third anniversary of the People of Hope. I had just been elected to lead the community. Following dinner, I was asked to speak. Heading to the microphone, I said a quick prayer and then began my remarks.

This evening I am grateful to the Lord for the comfort and courage He has given our family. Fourteen years ago today our son John-Paul was taken off life support because he had been brain dead for twenty-four hours. He was six-and-a-half and was killed in a car accident right in front of our house. There is rarely a day goes by that we don't think of him and pray to him. Whereas a night like this on the anniversary of his death would have been the most bitter of ironies a few short years ago—unthinkable, in fact—I now find the paradox of all this happening on the anniversary of his death to be poetic. It is almost as if he's saying; "I told you I would be with you!" From sorrow we thought would never end we can feel his presence and joy and laughter with us here tonight.

Why is that? I believe that it is because the resurrection of the Lord that we celebrate in this Easter season and the redemption He won for us on the Cross inexorably make their way, if we allow them, into the very fiber of our souls and convince us that life vanquishes death over and over again!

Why speak of John-Paul Floyd tonight? Because I am convinced by the words of St. Paul in Romans, chapter eight, ". . . neither death, nor life, nor angels, nor principalities, nor things present, nor things to come, nor powers, nor height, nor depth, nor anything else in all creation, will be able to separate us from the love of God in Christ Jesus our Lord (Romans 8:38–39 RSV)." Earlier in that passage St. Paul exclaims, "If God is for us, who is against us? He who did not spare his own Son but gave him up for us all, will he not also give us all things with him? . . . Who shall separate us from the love of Christ? Shall tribulation, or distress, or persecution, or famine, or nakedness, or peril or sword? . . . No, in all these things we are more than conquerors through him who loved us (Romans 8:31–32, 35, 37 RSV)."

Brothers and sisters, death cannot separate us from the love of Christ. Present things cannot separate us. Future things cannot separate us. Tribulation and distress cannot separate us. Persecution and famine cannot separate us. Nakedness and peril and the sword cannot separate us from the love of Christ. The present age cannot separate us. The rulers of the world cannot separate us. Losing our jobs cannot separate us. Losing our health, our wealth, our mental and physical faculties, our spouses, our children—nothing can separate us from the love of Christ. They can take us to the edge, where we can no longer depend on our own strength and resources, where everything we possess is simply not enough to get us through, but they cannot separate us.

On the contrary, God is so much the King and the Master and the Lord, that He uses everything—even the most difficult things, the bad things, the shameful things, the horrific things, even our sin (as Saint Paul points out in chapter five)—to draw us back to Himself. Indeed, as Saint Paul promised, He works all things to the good for those who love Him. Brothers and sisters, let us thank God, who is constantly working it all to the good for each one of us, in ways we often can't imagine and along paths we might never have chosen.

With these few words spoken, I sat down. Maureen took my hand and looked at me and we savored how much the Lord had done for us. We also knew that we were far away from the early stages of grief, and gratefully so.

In retrospect, what was significant for me about putting those words together? Simply this: words are signposts along a journey. We trace where we've come from by looking back. That is why Judaism and Christianity have a retrospective character as well as an ever-widening horizon of hope. We look back as well as forward. Remembering the mercies and the mighty deeds of the Lord gives us courage to move forward. As the psalmist tell us: "One generation shall laud thy works to another" (Ps. 145:4 RSV). Elsewhere we read: "Only take heed, and keep your soul diligently, lest you forget the things your eyes have seen, and lest they depart from your heart all the days of your life; make them known to your children and your children's children" (Deut. 4:9 RSV). As we have looked back over the years and seen the many ways in which the Lord has shown us mercy and compassion, we have ample reason to press on with confidence.

We have experienced much grace. Grace, however, builds upon nature, as St. Thomas Aquinas has taught us. Another key to our healing was dealing with the natural level as well as the spiritual.

2. NATURAL LIFE. At some point, for the insurance company, we needed to "prove" that we, and the children, were grieving. We were asked to take Gregory, Therese, and David to a counselor. I remember calling Eileen McGrath, the therapist who had been recommended to us, and saying to her, "Eileen, we're a Catholic family and we believe in the resurrection of the dead. We are dreadfully aware of how dead our son is and we also believe that he is alive and in heaven and that we're going to see him again. If you think that is simply a Freudian 'object of wish fulfillment' at work and that we are really just masking our grief I would prefer that you tell me now so we don't waste each other's time." After a moment's pause, a gentle voice responded: "Mr. Floyd, I'm a former nun. I, too, believe in the resurrection from the dead. I, too, believe that you will see your son again. And no, I don't believe that your hope in eternal life is a form of neurosis."

Eileen's specialty was dealing with grieving children. Meeting her was an introduction to a world of therapy that was compassionate and credentialed, truthful, hopeful, and grounded in reality—the reality that grief is a process. Eileen was a woman of faith and substance, and she told us things that were immensely helpful, things that were like rocks in the storm that was surging around us. After the second or third session, she pulled me aside. "Your kids are going to be OK," she said. "Don't be surprised if they hit some rough patches at different stages of their growth, but they are going to be OK. Why? Because you're letting them grieve and you're letting them see you grieve. You're allowing them to speak about the things going on inside them. You and Maureen are making it OK for them to say what's on their minds. You're validating their grief, even as it is very different from your own. And far from harming them, your grief allows them to see that they are just as loved as Johnny was."

Eileen's expert guidance was a gift.

Next it was our turn. Though I had respect for the help that the psychological sciences could offer, and had on occasion encouraged people to avail themselves of this help, counselors and counseling were not on my radar screen—at least for me and my family. Nonetheless, Maureen and I went to a counselor whose PhD was in thanatology, the study of death and grieving. Having worked with grieving individuals for thirty years, Gail Giacolone was in a position of some authority to know what worked and what didn't. I remember Maureen coming home from her first session, saying: "I felt more validated, understood, and affirmed in the first five minutes with Gail than from almost anything people have said to me since Johnny died." "What did she say?" I asked. "I can't believe you're still standing." That was it. But in that moment, Maureen experienced a woman who understood the profound human dimensions of her loss and its mental and physical consequences. Gail, also a woman of faith, told us about sleeping and eating and exercising and giving each other space and time. She told us that we would grieve in different ways and according to different timelines and that this was normal and to be expected. Everything she told us proved true. She had the experience. And even though we only went to see her a few times, she was immensely helpful and a key instrument in our healing.

Why mention this? I have found that sometimes, among men and women of faith, there is a suspicion about psychology, counseling, and therapy. No doubt there are reasons for this, bound up in bad experiences that people have had or have heard of. This suspicion is bound up with a sense that if you have Christ in your life, you should be able to handle whatever comes your way. That is true for many things. However, if more help can be given to someone who is suffering, would it not be more charitable and more reasonable to avail of that help? Some situations are more complicated. Finding the dead body of your son on your front lawn is different from struggling to get along with the deacon or the organist or the co-worker who gets on your nerves. Not everyone needs this kind of help. We probably wouldn't have gone to a counselor if we hadn't been required to. But going was a big assist that gave us practical pointers for moving forward.

Fifteen years later, I still imagine very bad things happening to our children. I imagine them being abducted, raped, abused, murdered. When I don't know where they are, I get anxious. I read Rose the riot act before she left for Spain for her senior year, telling her about everything from Rufenol (the date rape drug) to the white slave trade. Ditto for Susanna about walking to her car late at night on campus. I'm still on guard with the kids when it comes to parking lots, though less than I used to be. Years ago, I told Eileen about how stern I was with the kids in parking lots, because I was so fearful of them getting hit by a car and possibly killed. She responded: "Gregory, most kids don't die in parking lots. So when that thought comes, simply say, 'Cancel that thought.'" I have, many times since, "cancelled that thought."

Our few hours with these gifted therapists reaffirmed for me the fact that truth is symphonic. All truth simultaneously glorifies the Lord and lifts up the human person, whatever its origin. We were "lifted up" by the work of these two women and set on a road to healing. So yes, just as faith has staying power, counseling does, too. It goes without saying that finding the right therapist is key.

Living with an absence has left a hole that opens at unexpected moments. Maureen said to me on several occasions before David's wedding: "I don't know how I'm going to get down that aisle without him: he and Gregory would have walked me down the aisle together." But the day came, and like so many other days in the early years, the anticipation of it proved more difficult than the day itself. By the grace of God, we live with Johnny's presence as well as his absence. In the reality of the communion of the saints, we know that we are one in the Lord, one with those in heaven and those on earth. A few years after Johnny died, a friend sent me a quote by then Cardinal Joseph Ratzinger, now Pope Benedict XVI, which hangs above my desk to this day:

> We know that the souls of those who have died are alive in the resurrected body of the Lord. The Lord's Body shelters and carries them toward the common resurrection. In this Body, which we are permitted to receive in Holy Communion, we remain close to one another, and we touch each other.

With the passage of time I find I don't think about Johnny every day. This is hard to admit, but it's true. Certainly not more than a day goes by without my thinking of him, but his death is not a present reality to me in the way it was five or ten years ago. This is not a bad thing, though it is, at the same time, a letting go. This is something that would have been incomprehensible a few scant years ago. So much is so back to normal. Life is about the big kids who are now grown and the little kids who are growing up. It's about mortgages and colleges and loans and car repairs and leaky faucets and leaky roofs. It's about our own sin and our limitations. It's about continuing to forge a deeper unity with Maureen as we navigate the different changes and challenges in our life together.

After Johnny died people would occasionally talk to us about the spiritual warfare surrounding the death of a loved one. In my experience, we were spared that particular battle. It seemed that God had surrounded us with his biggest angels so that we could grieve in peace, without the torment of other, darker, spiritual forces. Years later, I realize that other issues still come back to haunt me that have nothing to do with Johnny. Among them is vulnerability to certain temptations.

One of those temptations is self-pity. I can recognize self-pity for what it is. I have found, on occasion, that when things are not going well, at work or at home, or when I am intimidated by someone or something, I am tempted to say to myself, "Yes, but you don't know what I've been through." As I have become aware of this temptation, I try not to think, "my life would be so much better if Johnny were here," when the truth is that I've got a problem to deal with.

Another temptation is alienation, an impulse to want to pull back because the rest of the world doesn't get what it feels like to lose a child. The fact is that the death of a child is alienating.

It pulls parents and siblings away from the common experience of most people. Most people, thank God, don't have to deal with such an experience. That is still no excuse for retreating from humanity.

A third temptation is wanting to repeat the war stories of the ignorant and insensitive things people said to us, or to remember the holes left by the things people didn't say.

These temptations, like all others, have no moral content. They are pieces of information that tell us something about ourselves: our weaknesses, our needs, our vulnerabilities, our idols. They have no power until we yield to them. For me, the problem of yielding to any of them, even if only in my mind, is that they blind me to the innumerable acts of kindness that people did show and the many words of comfort that people did offer. It's better to say, "I will not repeat that again."

3. OUR MARRIAGE. A great lesson we've learned over the years from the Franciscan priest Fr. Raniero Cantalamessa is that our children derive security not so much from the love they receive from us as from the love they witness between us. Psychologists say that the death of a child is the greatest stressor on a marriage. We have friends whose spouses left them because they could not handle the death of their child. Where are we now, fifteen years later?

We tell each other we're getting old! We kid each other about who gets to die first. While that might sound like a bit of gallows humor, it signifies a genuine longing for the day when this earthly life with its sorrows and disappointments and incompleteness will be over and we will be at home with the Lord. It also signifies a gift that God gave us when Johnny died that continues to this day: we do not fear death. Fifteen years later we still look at death as the great family reunion at which we will be united with him. Indeed, heaven is the heart's deepest longing, as the title of Peter Kreeft's book suggests. Meanwhile, I tell Maureen that with that figure of hers and eight adorable children in tow, men will be lining up at the door for the chance to propose!

While awaiting that day, we live here, in this present moment. Maureen asked me last December what I wanted for Christmas. I said, "Ballroom dancing lessons at the local high school." She didn't know if I was kidding. I said, "We're too busy, and we always have something we haven't gotten to. We're going to drop everything and go out for an hour a week to have fun." And so we did. Between foxtrots and waltzes and the jitterbug we were able to put everything on pause and simply enjoy each other's company. Those classes are over, and we have already forgotten most of what we learned, but not the memory of how much we enjoy spending time with each other.

We fight to create space and time for each other, because when we have un-rushed, undistracted time together, we are renewed in each other's presence. These encounters don't admit of precise timelines: one can't plan a "mutually revelatory" conversation, or a moment when deep vulnerability is met with unconditional love. At the same time, our commitment to meet weekly to talk about all the things going on in our lives and in the family provides the backdrop for them. The pressures of children still in grade school and high school and college and grad school and the constant stream of guests, school meetings, work commitments, and caring for others add up. What we've discovered is that we need even more time alone to talk things through in order to reach a deeper understanding of each other and of what we can, and should (and shouldn't), handle. We are trying much more deliberately to balance priorities, to ask each other, "Do you really need to do that?" or "Can someone else do that?"

In the midst of all the day-to-day needs and issues, however, the calls come. They are from someone who lost a child, or from the friend of someone who lost a child. Some are from far away or are about a tragedy that happened long ago. Some are as recent as the evening news. Several years back, we took the kids out for pizza on Johnny's anniversary. When we returned, there was a message on the phone. It was from a man from Michigan who had lost his son thirty-four years previously in a bus accident. He was calling to say that somehow he had come upon a copy of *A Grief Unveiled*. Reading it, he had finally found peace. That this call would have come on Johnny's anniversary is the kind of experience that we can only greet with silence and bowed heads. Three weeks ago Maureen received a call from the friend of woman in the next town whose son had been killed in a car accident shortly before Christmas. The woman asked if Maureen could meet with the bereaved mother. Of course, she said yes.

It costs Maureen to speak to someone who has lost a child. She will do it, because she knows she has some things to say that can really help people and that will give them hope. However, she needs to prepare for these moments in prayer. She will do whatever is needed, but it wouldn't be her preference to talk frequently about Johnny's death: for her to do so is to revisit the old pictures and the old sorrow. That being said, she is fully present if someone who lost a child wants to talk. If there's a need she can meet from someone across town or someone across the country, a relative or friend, she does so without hesitation. She has not lost the ability to get way out of her comfort zone in order to serve. We've had people show up at the door or call and ask if they could visit. I think they just want to see somebody who made it through. They want to know that life will continue despite their loss, and, especially in the early months, that the pain, isolation, and bewilderment that accompany early grief will someday subside. She can tell them it will.

In the past two years, both of my parents died. After my mother's Alzheimer's and my father's dementia, Maureen asks me if I'm worried that I will lose my mind. Having watched my mother lose hers (that seems to be literally what happens with Alzheimer's: the progressive losing of one's mind, piece by piece; no wonder the Irish call it "the long good-bye"), the thought that this could happen to me is not one I relish. At the same time, I recognize that there's nothing I can do about it and that worrying won't help, and may even advance it! So I tell her she's stuck with me whether I do or I don't. She tells me she will be there. We have learned that, united in Christ and in the grace of the sacrament of marriage, we can face anything together. We can look at the trials that come our way and say, "We've been through worse." It gives us a certain bottom line approach to the challenges of daily living as well as the unexpected difficulties.

We have grown in letting our preferences and differences of approach be visible to each other. We are different: two sets of gifts with two corresponding sets of limitations. We can disagree and realize that we're viewing reality from two different sides of a prism and that we don't, and can't, see everything from the same vantage point. When we're on our game, we pull one another to the center, where Christ is. But we are one. We are encountering new moments of growth in learning to accept and respect each other's strengths and limitations. We're regularly challenged by our pace of life and our service. We recognize anew the cost of having a large family. These aren't problems, they are simply challenges that we said yes to a long time ago.

4. OUR FAMILY. Our biggest concern in the early years was the children. How would they do? This was a natural question, since we were in uncharted territory. Our most fundamental response to how they are doing is humble gratitude to the Lord who loves them far more than we do. From having just had Nicole six weeks prior to Johnny's death, we went on to be blessed with two other daughters, Katie and Maria. The three of them and their five older siblings are marked by their experience of Johnny's death. Even the ones who were very little, and the ones who were not yet born, are marked. While the intense emotions have softened and quieted over the course of time, Johnny is never far from their minds.

His death is a reality that is not sewn up for them. It is not something neatly packaged and gloriously resolved. Their theology needs development, but even their questioning, as they've gotten older, is a kind of proof of the existence of God: they are calling out to Someone for answers. They have suffered. The ones who knew him have suffered and the ones who did not know him have suffered. There is a residual anger that surfaces in their writing, a crying out against the unfairness of why this happened to Johnny, to our family, and to each of them as individuals. At the same time, other recurring themes emerge. They are filled with hope: the eschatological and uniquely Christian hope that they will see him again. They are surer of this than anything else. They are sure they have a brother in heaven praying for them. Several of them have been drawn to different kinds of service, particularly to the poor and marginalized. They attribute this, in part, to his impact on their lives. After all, Johnny was the one who prayed every night for the children who were poor and didn't have anything to eat.

They have come to understand the unique gift of being a family, for all our sin and imperfections. We told them that life would get better, that it wouldn't always feel like it did in the early days and months. Life has gotten better, and they know that they are better, much better, for his brief years with us. We all know we would live life with Johnny all over again if we could, if by some terrifying premonition we could repeat the exact same six-year scenario. Johnny's death has given them, and us, us a more realistic and temperate view of life: of its dramatic limitations as well as its incandescent moments of grace. We are learning not to expect more of it than it is designed to give. After all, this life is meant to point us beyond itself to the true and unending life of heaven.

This more measured view helped us to engage the sickness and deaths of my mother and father, and the mental diminishment that afflicted them. Mom had her Master's degree from Columbia University and had begun her PhD thesis on the Renaissance of Christian Humanism in twentieth-century French literature at the University of Strasbourg in France. Mom came into a deep, personal relationship with the Lord through the charismatic renewal and spent years leading women's Bible studies. Mom could entertain five or ten at a moment's notice and make it look effortless. Mom did everything from campfire breakfasts to taking us to museums and concerts. This same Mom, over the course of the relentless robbery of her brain by Alzheimer's, was reduced to talking about the moon as the "round thing in the sky." A little later she was reduced to calling us all "Love," because she could no longer remember our names. The woman who made my high school friends and me laugh by donning a black turtleneck and leotard and dancing around the kitchen to Debussy's *The Afternoon of a Faun* was reduced to being moved about in a wheelchair. And this woman, always so elegant without the slightest trace of snobbery, was reduced to having her matted gray hair cut off and combed back "boy style" because she wouldn't let people get near her with scissors and machines. She was dressed in formless clothes with snaps and the like because she didn't want people dressing her. Bathing was scary for her. I used to feel terrible for her: she had grown up in a much more modest culture. To have people take her clothes off and bathe her was a torment, especially when she could no longer understand that people were trying to help her.

And yet, as she was in the midst of losing her mind, we would pray together when Maureen or I visited her. She would surprise us with rare moments of utter lucidity. Once as we were praying, when she could no longer string even a few words together, she said: "Lord, give the boys courage and confidence for the things that will confront them." In that brief prayer I realized how the legacy of faith is passed from one generation to the next.

Mom died in January of 2011. I always thought it sounded odd when people said of the person in the casket: "She looks good." My reaction was always, "No, she looks dead." I was surprised at my own relief when her wake came. With her hair done, and dressed in a beautiful suit, she finally looked like the woman I had spent my life with. But with all that said, losing Mom was not the same as losing Johnny.

Although Dad had died ten months before Mom, in March of 2010, her mental decline was much more precipitous than his and figured much more prominently in her care by the whole family. However, as Mom was succumbing to Alzheimer's, Dad began his battle with dementia. The man who won a

213

basketball scholarship to college fell and got 150 stitches in his face. The man who was a spy in World War II, parachuting behind enemy lines in France and China, couldn't find his way back to their condo in their small New Jersey town. Dad, who could balance his checkbook to the penny in March, could not figure it out in April. The man who was so protective of Mom took her, and all his papers, on a cold November day with neither of them sufficiently dressed, on a walk to an office that didn't exist, to register to vote. A friend of ours saw them on the road, confused, and drove them home. We mourned their deaths, and we miss them: their presence, their support, their thoughtfulness, their laughter and their wisdom, their faith and their love. But the quality of grief surrounding their deaths, real as it was, was different. It is in the realm of nature for children to bury their parents, not the opposite.

Now more than fifteen years later, after the death of Johnny, a miscarriage, and the deaths of my parents, we recognize that life is a precious gift whose length is unknown to us. While we can't be at our children's beck and call, we also don't want to hold back on giving them our attention, love, wisdom, experience, compassion, and time. We realize they thrive on affection and that we all suffer, to some degree, from "affirmation deprivation neurosis" (a theory proposed by the Dutch psychiatrist Conrad Baars). We try to tell them often that we love them and show it with affection, because if things become implicit for too long ("they know we love them"), they disappear.

We know they need us and not things. We know we have enormous influence on them, more than anything or anyone else in their lives. We know that we are not required to keep them busy and amused. We need to teach them to work and create opportunities for them to serve. We've come to see that we're always modeling, always communicating. Whether it's love, anger, disinterest, impatience, boredom, stress, joy, kindness, enthusiasm, or whatever, we're always communicating. We hope and pray that we're leaving them a legacy of faith and love.

5. FRIENDSHIP AND COMMUNITY. The treasure of living in committed relationships in the Christian community of the People of Hope has enormous staying power. While many things have come and gone, this has remained. The same friends who walked with us in the early years after Johnny's death walk with us today. We now walk together to the funerals of one another's parents and to the weddings of one another's children. On rare occasions, we walk, more slowly and more quietly, to the funerals of one another's children. We know that we have been here for each other and we will continue to be here for each other. Johnny's godparents never let a birthday go by without flowers or a plate of cookies appearing at the door. It is the same with Maureen's sister Nancy and her husband JJ: there's always a card, a call and, last year, dinner and a ball game at Yankee Stadium. Thoughtfulness surrounds us. The Clementes, without fail, call both of us and speak to us of the boy they loved so much. They still have Johnny's picture on their fridge. Several other friends do the same. Fifteen years out we are still occasionally surprised by the impact of his death: just last year one friend told me that his adult daughter doesn't like the smell of certain flowers because they remind her too much of Johnny's wake: she was one of his close friends in kindergarten! This kind of personal support is the gift of Christian community in this time. In the midst of a culture so exhausted by individualism, isolation, and alienation, we are bound together by an invitation from the Lord to love one another. It affects everything. We are bound together by time: by many years of loving, forgiving, forbearing, and sharing life and the deep healing that this kind of relational stability brings. We are bound together by space: we have decided to live here, at this time and in this place, and to be present to one another in ways that transcend the selectivity of our personal likes and dislikes. We are bound together by a call: the call to be a community, to be disciples, to be on mission whether we are on Main Street or Wall Street or the college campus or the laundry room. We are bound together by memory: the collective memory of what God has done among us as well as the memory of what has happened to us and to each other. And we are bound together by hope: the biblical hope that assures us that we are not alone, that victory over sin and death has been won and that one day there will be no more tears or crying out, no more horror and shock, no more disaster. We help each other remember and we help each other to hope.

Over the years, as the community has aged and more and more dear friends have died, we have learned to give grieving its time, to honor the season that it imposes on us. For all the signs of God's kingdom and the indwelling of His Holy Spirit that are so powerfully a part of the communities and movements that God has raised up around the world, there is still a necessary trajectory of human growth and development that grounds and enriches and integrates these experiences of His gratuitous love. Grace comes to us to make us "more human" if that were possible, or, at least, truly human, as Christ is. In the end, it is a gift beyond compare to have these relationships that call us to live the truth, to remember, and to hope.

6. RITUALS. I take every April 24th as a personal day. Maureen and I get up, go to Mass, and then head to the beach as soon as the kids have gone to school. We sit at the ocean, we talk, and we rest. At 3:20 we pause and pray. It is quiet; it is sometimes wistful, but it is not excruciating. On April 24th, we are glad we are getting older. On Johnny's baptismal day, we still make his favorite meal for the children: pizza and nachos, and we tell Johnny stories. On Good Friday we take flowers to his gravesite and plant them. Then we each pray to him because our son and brother is with the Lord and we hope he is whispering into God's ear on our behalf. On Christmas Maureen hangs the wooden Christmas stocking that he made in kindergarten with his photograph on it. He is there, all six-and-a-half glorious years of him. These rituals mark a life, not a death. They give us time to pause and remember. We are grateful for the memories.

TWENTY

The Kids Weigh In

When I was asked to write for the new edition of *A Grief Unveiled*, I thought it would be helpul for each of the children to write as well. I told them they did not have to write—that it was an invitation; not a command performance—but all eight decided they wanted to add their thoughts to mine. What follows is their reflections of the years that followed Johnny's death.

GREGORY
27 years old. He was 10 when Johnny died.

I think *time* is what's hard. That it doesn't stop. That it doesn't change. That it isn't somehow marked by the death of a child, by the death of my brother. That Johnny now lives in a time beyond, a time apart—a time that rarely, if ever, intersects with our own. And with each passing anniversary the disproportion grows between the brief years he was with us and the long years since. I can't help thinking that we forget things in those intervening years. Because alongside the disinterested march of time is our daily living. We go on to high school, to college, to Europe. We graduate and begin careers. And suddenly Johnny, his life and his death, seem not only separated by years, but also as if they were in another lifetime. There are memories that stand the test of time: long weekday afternoons playing in the woods and the backyard, swimming out beyond our depth with Dad and Pop at the beach, the particularly deep shade of crimson he turned when he was embarrassed, and, of course, his laughter. But there are others that grow dim and some even that fade.

It has always been hard not to know how to talk about Johnny's death with friends—both those who knew him and those whom I've come to know and love since his death. With people who knew Johnny we can talk about him, laugh at many happy memories, and speak about sadness and pain, but I'm not sure we can, for all that, really share one another's grief, though we all grieve. I think grief is indeed a solitary walk. And for those friends I've come to know since, when do you share this significant and defining experience? When they correct you for miscounting the number of your siblings? When they ask, as someone did recently, if you've experienced suffering in your life? No, there is no natural way into that conversation. Yet, it remains a conversation that must be had, because Johnny's life and death and continued presence are part of our family and part of my life.

The University of Notre Dame has an outdoor "Grotto" modeled on the holy site in Lourdes, France. It is a popular place for students to take a moment and reflect or utter a few Hail Marys, especially around exam time. I remember sitting at the Grotto during my junior year of college on April 24th, having asked a friend to come with me. I told him that it was Johnny's anniversary. I don't think we talked about it then. I'm not sure we've talked about it since. But it felt wrong that the day should go by unmarked and unacknowledged, as if it were any other Monday in April.

But there are also moments of proximity and moments of presence. Despite the fact that daily life moves on and Johnny now lives in a time beyond, there are moments when the two worlds touch, when he is near. You can't plan for it, but suddenly it's there, an unmistakable presence. It can happen at times of family celebration. It can happen in times of grief. He was a palpable presence during the deaths of both my dad's parents. It can happen in times of prayer. And it can also happen in times of idle speculation: What would he have looked like? What would his temperament have been like? What would he have studied? Where? What would our relationship have become? These moments are often provoked by unexpected encounters with his friends and classmates who are now adults themselves. I wonder what might have been and how my life would have been different because of it.

No one teaches you how to grieve. Grief can't only be a question of the intense emotion felt at the outset because that recedes over time. I have found that grief is learning how to live with an absence. I'm still not sure I know how to do this. At times I waiver between regretting that my life hasn't stopped its involvement with the cares of daily life on the one hand, and, on the other, I worry that I am trying to invest memories and feelings with a significance or fullness that perhaps they can't.

In the end, I guess I still don't know what to do with the brute fact that Johnny was alive on Easter Sunday and dead on Easter Monday. This is not a problem that can be solved or thought through; it's not a relationship that can be mended with repentance and forgiveness; it is not a wound to be healed, if by that we mean "cured." It's living with an absence. It's a "thing," an object, but not one you can grab hold of and inspect. It's a space, an empty space that I crawl into from time to time to think about its dimensions and vacuity, its lack of intelligibility and brute facticity. In the end, grief, I think, is simply a collection of ways of relating to someone who is no longer there. I've come to think of it as a set of behaviors without any correct order or priority. Powerful emotions, happy memories, wistful thinking, prayerful reflection—these are all ways of keeping Johnny close so that, even though he can't be fully present to us, he can still be close by.

Johnny's death has taught me that there are some questions we cannot answer, at least on this side of the veil. And yet we must continue to live. But in living with such a paradox, we live with a certain degree of restlessness and vulnerability. We live with the knowledge that all is not right, that all cannot be put back as it once was. And yet to this our faith responds that "all will be well" and promises with Christ that those who mourn are "blessed," that they will be comforted, and, indeed, one day laugh. And so we live with hope.

Looking back on these last fifteen years, I realize that I've had to confront Johnny's death and my own grief at various moments in my growth from early adolescence into adulthood. When Johnny died I felt a tremendous sense of responsibility for my family. I had to be strong. I had to help hold things together. I had to carry on the story at the dinner table or the prayer at the graveyard when someone's voice broke. I felt guilty that my sense of loss didn't appear as profound as that of my parents. Perhaps I hadn't loved Johnny enough. I can remember the first night I slept in Johnny's bed as Dave's new roommate. We both just lay there in silence.

I can remember another moment five or six years later. I was a junior in high school and was out for a walk with my dad. I can remember confiding in him that Johnny's death had changed me. I had begun to realize that I approached situations and thought about things differently from many of my friends.

My world was different, not better or worse, just different. I felt at times that I had been asked to grow up too fast. Now as an adult, I often wonder if my impulse toward service work was somehow tied to these early experiences, an attempt to set things right in the world, and then perhaps in my own heart. Thankfully, though my parents' sorrow was and remains inscrutable to me, they were very attentive to us following the accident. My siblings and I were given opportunities to speak and to grieve.

A third moment that comes to mind occurred during my freshman year of college. I remember thinking as I prepared to move halfway across the country that it was important to bring a copy of *A Grief Unveiled* with me. I couldn't say why. I don't even think I had read it cover to cover. Like many of my books, it sat in a corner of my dorm room for the fall semester. But I remember picking it up during the spring semester and thinking I ought to read through it. It had been almost ten years since Johnny's death. Unfortunately, I chose a crowded student center in the middle of the day to start my reading. After about five pages I had to shut the book, compose myself, and then dart back across campus to the privacy of my dorm room. Everything had come back in a flash. Feelings and memories I hadn't had in years, some in almost a decade, seemed to have happened only yesterday. Strange though it may seem, this experience was comforting. It put me back in touch with my own grief and with the fact that I loved Johnny, and that I missed him. I realized that no matter how many intervening years there were or how many important milestones were reached, he remained a part of our family.

Johnny's death has brought our family closer together. It has taught us to value one another and our relationships more. To live with grief is to live exposed, not only to suffering, but also to love. In vulnerability it opens us outward to others. In hope it opens us outward to eternity and the promise that we will see him again. In the end, time will continue to march on and memories will fade, but faith can make the one who is absent present. And this faith allows us, allows me, to live in hope.

THÉRÈSE
25 years old. She was 9 when Johnny died.

We didn't have a choice to keep Johnny or not. He was taken. That is the hardest struggle for me. Having worked in the missions in Honduras and currently in pediatric oncology, I am confronted with the loss of people I love. No matter how much I love, I can't love someone into living. That's why without hope, life doesn't make any sense: hope that there is a bigger picture, hope that God is love and truly will hold us. My whole life is colored by losing Johnny. Our family is changed. I think we hold each other all the more closely knowing what it is like to lose someone. I am fiercely protective of my siblings.

I am a pediatric nurse. I knew from the beginning that I would either run from pediatrics like it was on fire, or fall so hard that I couldn't do much else. I fell. I am oddly comfortable around suffering. I can stand quietly in the corner or hold a patient or his or her loved one as they collapse in pain and grief. I can be friends with those in what we call "the club no one wants to join." Where does this confidence and ease come from? From losing Johnny. From needing to find a place to put all the feelings of grief and pain and horror and turning them into something that can help someone else. I didn't have a choice about whether I would deal with Johnny's death or not. I needed to make some sense out of it. To me, death wins if I hide in a room and let anger rule my life. I owe it to Johnny to make my life count for more than that. I find comfort in shouldering a burden, like so many others did for me. Most of my patients and their families never know I see myself or my family in them. I pray that I exude a sense of hope and love as I walk alongside them.

I think I have learned to love. I don't have control over how long I will have someone, so if this is my moment with him or her, I want it to count! It hurts to love: people let you down. You let people down. But it's so worth it! Love changes lives. Johnny's love changed mine. His light shone so brightly that others found their own light by seeing his. I have begun to find my own light. I want to leave this world spent, knowing I gave all I had. I pray that when someone hears our story and sees ten survivors who can stand straight and are for the most part pretty well adjusted, who have each taken this cross and responded to it, then they, too, will have hope.

God is good. I know He didn't wish this upon me. He wasn't punishing me, and he never wants to hurt me. Nonetheless, it happened, and I have had to ask Him lots of questions and, on occasion, demand some answers (knowing, of course, that I cannot demand that the Lord of the universe answer my questions!). Some answers will not come until the other side of death. God probably rolls his eyes when He hears my call bell—but He never fails to acknowledge it. Though He hasn't always given me answers I liked or wanted, feeling abandoned by Him was never an issue. He has been quiet as I, at times, have ranted. But He never left me alone. When I come to really hard situations at work or in life, I feel like He and I are a team. We have come this far and I know He will see me through. Sometimes I feel worn, and I'm only 25! But it's not a bad *worn*; it's like resting in a valley before the next climb. You know you made one climb, and you're still feeling its effects, and you know there are many more to come. But you have confidence that He will see you though.

After finishing nursing school in 2007, I spent a year as a missionary in Honduras. There, without a lot of the comforts and relationships of home, I had a chance to look at my life. Many times during that year Johnny's death would catch me so off guard that the feeling was physical, as though someone had punched me in the gut. As I strived, during that year, to become more and more who God created me to be—daughter, sister, nurse, missionary, and friend—I realized that Johnny had accomplished everything he was supposed to in six and a half years. Nonetheless, I am frequently struck by the void, the space, the relationship that he was supposed to fill.

Many instances come to mind. Greg and Dave stood together at Summerfest, a gathering of young people from our community: he should have been there with them. The "big kids" went out before I moved to Honduras: he was missing. I brought the "first guy home" and he wasn't there to give me grief about it. Rose went to college and he wasn't there to give her brotherly advice. Dave and their childhood friend Mike traveled through Europe, and while I'm sure he watched over them, he wasn't physically there. Greg is giving retreats to his classmates but the class is one too few. The little girls keep growing and he is only a memory. What a loss!

Suffering escapes no one. I think that through the brokenness and pain of losing him, I have become more open. I picture the wounds that come from his absence more as "holes" in my heart to let love pour out. I want to give, because I know what it is to lack. I am stunned by the number of lives my brother touched in so few years.

I remember one day in Honduras; it was the anniversary of Johnny's death. I had wanted to feel close to him because I was really missing him. Driving to Tegucigalpa to renew my visa and take a friend to the airport, we passed a traffic accident and saw a car stopped in the middle of the road and a young body lying in front of it. My friend and I got out. I stood in a similar spot to the one I had stood in years earlier. I took the pulse of a boy named José who was two years old and had just been hit by a car. José was dead on the road. I touched his hand while my friend prayed with him, my tears mixing with his blood. I had one thought that kept going through my mind: Somewhere in Comayagua there is a mother and a family who are breathing normally. They can take deep breaths from the bottom of their lungs. In twenty minutes when they hear this news they will no longer be able to do that. All I could think of was how I could make those twenty minutes last longer. What could I do so that this mother wouldn't have to hear that her son is dead? How could I make time stand still? I couldn't. I was overwhelmed by feeling the weight of their burden, the lot they didn't choose. This was way too close to home.

Back in the States the past few years, I have thought about moving forward, about getting married and having kids. Johnny, they will know about you! Just like we have told Katie and Maria who never met you in this life, you will mark their lives too! Through losing you, I long for something more than this limited world. Oh how I await that reunion in heaven where Dad and Mom will hold us all in their arms and once again present us to God as their treasure. Whole. Meanwhile, I pray that my heart always be "soft" to those in my path who are suffering. And until I see you again, Johnny, I love you and I let you go. But I hold onto hope, and the knowledge that without a doubt I will see you again!

DAVID
24 years old. He was 7 when Johnny died.
David was hit with Johnny, but survived.

The adage "Time heals all wounds" has never resonated with me. The finality of wounds "healing" suggests that things return to where they were. This has not happened to me since Johnny's death nor do I believe it ever will. The indelible mark that death leaves on the soul and the psyche seems to continually call me back to a frustratingly resounding "Why?" Why us? Why Johnny? Why me? I have found that as death continues to resurface in my own life, whether through the expected passing of my dad's parents the sudden passing of a friend's father, or random, insensible acts of violence, the question continues to hound me.

My understanding of Johnny's death is by no means complete. However, I think that reflecting on certain moments of my journey toward healing allows me to see that the path from pain to surrender is neither continuously upward nor crushing. I found comfort when I was willing to receive it.

As a seven-year-old, I was ill prepared to deal with death on either an intellectual level or an emotional one. It was difficult to process what exactly it meant for Johnny to be no more. As I moved through my teenage years, my inability to truly engage his death left me as somewhat of a ticking time bomb. While I thought about Johnny during my teenage years, I do not remember truly opening up the wounds for healing. On one hand, I thought that as a good Christian, I was supposed to accept that this had happened and trust in a greater vision that my fallible human mind could not grasp. Yet I knew within my heart of hearts that this was not enough for me. What was

I supposed to do? Question almighty God and call for some sort of response? This seemed borderline blasphemous to me and thus I buried it. It was a daunting thought to feel that God "owed" me something in terms of response or explanation.

As a freshman in college, I was seeking spiritual support and decided to attend a weekend retreat. Listening to one particular student offer a reflection on her father's death gave me pause for reflection. As I began writing in my journal, I found that I was angry, confused, and inconsolable. Having expected to spend ten minutes journaling, I found myself suddenly on the phone with my parents in a fit of grief and tears as the reality of "Why?" arose again. As I have reflected on this moment, I believe that a pattern was beginning to form in my own life. I had been called to deal with Johnny's death as a young boy, and now, as I entered a new stage as a young man beginning college, I was being called to deal with this pain in a new way.

From this time onward, my moments spent reflecting on Johnny's death were not accompanied by the same strong emotions. The next time I recall truly experiencing sorrow was in Cordoba, Spain. Having spent my junior year of college abroad, I traveled through the south of Spain by myself for a week, visiting churches, touring cities, and learning to hear my own voice again. I had found that being constantly surrounded by friends tended to reinforce certain self-images that may not have been accurate. I wanted to get away from friends for a time to get back to the core of who I am. In light of this, I perhaps should not have been surprised that Johnny's death rose to the forefront of my mind.

As I sat in a 500-year-old church meditating on the cross, a familiar verse rang through my mind: "The Lord hears the cry of the poor. Blessed be the Lord." I have never quite understood this verse, since my experiences have brought me to places where I have struggled to see the reality of God hearing that cry. Yet as this verse rang in my mind, I came to recognize myself as the poor, as the broken one, the one in search of being heard by the Lord, of being comforted by the God I was supposed to call "Abba."

Feelings of frustration and uncertainty about my deeper questions continued into my senior year of college. As I narrowed my focus for my senior thesis, I began to consider the relationship that I was called to have with God. As I reasoned, meaningful relationships have accountability. I fulfill my end of the covenant and God fulfills His. I felt that I had led a good life up that point as a faithful young man. Yet I could not see beyond the moment of Johnny's death to consider how God had fulfilled His end of the covenant. In my relationship with God, I had been seeking comfort and peace and had yet to find it in a lasting sort of way. I could connect with the bloody and broken body of Christ or the intimate touch of Mother Mary but I found the image of God to be cold, distant, and untouchable.

As I reflect back now, I think my arguments became an intellectual game of sorts, where a genuine search for God and understanding turned into a god of its own. The pursuit moved away from its source of inspiration, that being my own pain, and clouded what began as a genuine desire to heal. I cannot pinpoint the moment where I decided to give up my stubbornness and demands for accountability. However, I do know that it is terribly exhausting to stay angry with God. Beyond that, any attempt at spiritual development feels somewhat fraudulent. Moving past this pain, there are certain things I have come to hold as truths, and these are what anchor me in my times of doubt and darkness.

First, I have come to see that God has indeed been there. My genuine desire to continue to grow in holiness and virtue is "proof" enough that God does reach out to us in a very real way. Second, I recognize God's love and care mediated through various people. Whether through the comfort of my family or, now, the love of my wife, these sources of comfort are the responses to my pain and the attempts to make me whole that I have longed for since Johnny's death. Finally, I have come to see that my attempt to fit God into an intellectual framework is the wrong approach. Allowing myself to be continually surprised by God's love and goodness is much more refreshing and life-giving than a stubborn obstinacy in the face of grief.

What does it mean that I am the one who lived while Johnny died? I'm not quite sure. The question has weighed heavily on me. I try not to think about it, since I find that nothing I have done seems to justify my continued earthly existence in light of Johnny's death. I know that there is still something to be uncovered here. I know this because of the emotional response I have each time I linger in thinking or talking about Johnny. I believe that there is still more of the mystery surrounding his death and my life for me to uncover. I am sure it will come at a time when only goodness and healing will result. For now, my hope is to keep close the words of Christ: "I make all things new." As I continue to long for my brother, I hope in a renewal that may not come in this life but will surely come in the next.

ROSE
21 years old. She was 5 when Johnny died.

I don't think I can say that on April 24, 1995, my whole world came crashing down and that I was overtaken with grief. The fact is, I don't really remember that day. I have vivid memories of Johnny as he chased me around the house trying to steal my enormous roll of "bubble gum tape," but I don't remember the family and friends who came vigilantly to our house in those first days, nor the overwhelming sadness that must have enveloped everyone who walked though our door. However, despite the fact that I don't remember that specific day, the absence of a brother, especially one so close in age, is not something I could ever forget.

I vividly remember the first time I truly realized the impact that Johnny's death had left upon me. I was a sophomore in high school, fifteen years old. David had just left for college, and with Therese and Greg already in college, I was left at home with my parents and four younger sisters. The "little girls" were 12, 10, 8, and 5. Realizing that my older siblings were no longer home and that my younger siblings were too young to hang out with, I found myself alone for the first time in my life. Since I come from a family of nine kids, one would think that an impossibility. But as I thought more and more about my position in the family lineup, Johnny started coming to mind more and more as well. He was eighteen months older than me. If he hadn't died, he'd still be here with me; I could hang out with him and his friends and not have to be "stuck" at home. I wanted nothing more than for him to be back with us, with me, right then and there. But he wasn't. And the more I thought about it, the angrier I became.

The "why's" and the "what if's" started flooding my mind. What if the car had gone a little faster or a little slower? What if it had been raining that day and he and Dave hadn't been able to go outside? Why Johnny? Why my family? Why couldn't it have happened to someone else? With each question that popped into my mind I found myself getting more upset, more alone, and just plain angrier—at the situation, and at God for allowing it to happen. Instead of addressing everything I was thinking and feeling, I simply shut down.

I am not a "feelings" type of person. I don't like to talk about my feelings; I get over things quickly and it takes a lot to make me angry. I am not the best at letting others in, and I hate it when people know I'm sad or I'm having a hard time with something. I guess you could also say I'm a pretty stubborn person, but in that stubbornness is the competitive part of me, the part that thinks, or in this case thought, I could do everything by myself. In those first moments when I realized how angry and alone I really was, I told myself that everything would be fine; I'd get over it. No one would see that I was upset and hurt; no one would see that I was "weak." For whatever reason, I made myself believe that if I showed people that I was only now grieving and that it hurt so much, they would see me as weak. So instead of talking to someone about what I found myself going through, I bottled everything up inside and pretended that everything was normal.

In the beginning, I went along with the flow and did everything I was supposed to, but that did not last long. After a short time, my anger and frustration began to get the best of me. I had a very short temper and would snap back at people more and more often, usually my parents and little sisters. No one could have a conversation with me, since one-word answers don't get you very far. The attitude that accompanied the answers didn't help either. This was my way of dealing with everything. I, who didn't need any help and who could do everything on my own, couldn't bear the thought of people knowing I was broken and hurt. I was absolutely miserable. So I tried the one thing that I hadn't: I talked about it.

I had sworn to myself that I wasn't going to talk about Johnny's death; I would handle it on my own. Looking back,

I think I knew all along that I would not be able to carry this burden by myself. I would need help. I would need faith, family, and friends to support me. When I finally let them in, let them past all the walls I'd put up, I realized that it was OK for me to be sad. Being frustrated and upset at the death of my brother did not make me weak, but human. In the midst of a heated argument with my parents, I let everything out: the hurt, the anger, the frustration, and the loneliness. I don't think I really meant to let everything out, but I also don't think I could have held it in any longer. I told them about all the thoughts and feelings that I had had over the past weeks and months, and it was the greatest relief to finally get everything off my chest, to not have to deal with everything by myself anymore. In that moment, I truly began a healing process. It didn't happen right away, but over the next few years as I learned to accept and live with Johnny's death and understand what his death meant for me as a member of my family and as an individual. While at one point it seemed absolutely impossible to find the good in an awful situation, I began to learn how to do that. I started to actually see and believe that God did not allow this event to happen out of spite for me or my family, but because He had something better waiting for my brother. Do I still wish Johnny were here? Absolutely, every single day. But do I also realize that I have my own personal big-brother-guardian-angel-saint up in heaven watching out for me always and everywhere I go? Absolutely, every single day.

I think about Johnny a lot. Especially in the last few years, he's been on my mind more and more. Sometimes this makes me miss him more than I thought possible, and other times it's comforting to be able to go to his grave, talk to him, tell him what's going on, and ask him for advice, especially when I'm not really sure who else to go to. The loss of a brother, or of any close friend or family member, is probably the single most horrific thing that a person should have to deal with. There is so much pain and sorrow, so many unanswered questions. Yet I have come to believe that there is beauty that comes from pain. Whether we see it or not in a given moment, it is there and when the time comes that we are actually willing and able to search for it, we will find it. It may have taken me more than ten years to find it, but I did, and I see it every day when I say good morning to my personal angel in heaven.

SUSANNA
18 years old. She was almost 2 when Johnny died.

I think it is weird that you can really miss someone whom you knew so little about. I was only one and a half when my brother Johnny died, yet I miss him every single day. It is hard to believe he has been gone for fifteen years. With the passing of his birthday, baptismal day, and anniversary every year, I recall stories about him and his famous one-liners, which cause me to laugh or cry or sometimes do both. The pain that accompanies his death is something that is hard to describe, especially for me. Being so little when he passed away, I didn't grieve openly because I was too young to understand what was going on and did not remember him well. However, as I grew and continue to grow older, the fact that I did not know him well has made my grief that much greater, because he was gone before I could really get to know him. I hear the stories of how he loved me—how he held me in his arms and kissed my cheeks—and my eyes well up with tears. I wish I had memories with him that I could conjure up when I see his picture on the wall in our living room or when we are eating pizza and nachos and telling our favorite memories of him on his birthday.

Sometimes I am consumed with resentment and anger at the injustice of the situation. It's not fair. He was so young and had so much ahead of him, and all that was taken away in a second. I hate the fact that I never got to know him. He never taught me how to throw a punch, hit a baseball, or win an arm wrestle. We never played Power Rangers, G.I. Joes or waffle blocks. We never got the chance. How is that OK? How do I come to terms with and accept the death of an innocent child? How do I reconcile that with the goodness and power of God?

It's hard sometimes to hear other people outside of my family talk about him; I'm jealous that they can remember things about him and I can't. Sometimes I would give anything for a memory of him, to remember the sound of his voice, or to hear his laughter. It is in these moments of wanting to hear him and see him, that grief grips me so tightly. And yet, with each passing year and the different milestones our family reaches, Johnny's memory and presence are never far away.

It is the hope of life beyond the limitations of earth that gives me strength. In those moments when anger takes hold of my heart, all I can do is surrender to Christ (something more easily spoken about than done!). Yet, I cling to the truth of Christ's redemption and promise of salvation because that is the only way I will get to see my brother again. I know that he is there ahead of me, in the eternal happiness of heaven. When my time comes, I want to see his face waiting at the gates, his arm outstretched, ready to grasp my hand and guide me into eternity.

I love my brother John-Paul. Even though he was only here for a short period of my life, he has impacted me profoundly and has helped shape me into the person I am today. So many of my successes and triumphs are due to the prayers and intercessions of my big brother in heaven. Keep looking out for me, Johnny. I love you forever.

NICOLE
16 years old. She was only 6 weeks old when Johnny died.

When my father invited me to write this, I was actually looking forward to sharing some of my thoughts about Johnny. Yet when I sat down to write something, I didn't know what to say. It's not that I didn't have anything to say; it was rather that there was so much confusion in my mind. I didn't want to sound angry or bitter, or that I just accepted everything that had happened. There was such a mix of emotions. I talked to a wise teacher of mine, and he told me that I needed to be real and that the way I dealt with Johnny's death was personal. I know that the way I deal with his death is not the same as that of any of my other family members. Each of us occupies a unique place in the family, and therefore I wouldn't deal with Johnny's death the same way my mother or father or siblings do, because they have a different position than I do.

I write from the point of view of a sister who has grieved the loss of a brother. The hardest thing is that I don't know Johnny. I don't know my brother. I have heard stories and I have seen his picture, but to say I know my brother? On a personal level? Sadly, that's not true.

Growing up, Johnny was always a part of my life. He was always my big brother up in heaven. We always talked about Johnny and it was always a happy thing. I was too young to conceptualize in my mind that it was something horrific that had taken my brother away from me. As I grew older, I could understand the gravity of the situation. I had a brother who died in a car accident when he was six years old and I was six weeks old, and I never knew him. I have not one personal memory of him, but I desperately wanted one, one I could hold onto. It's hard to claim you know someone when you can only piece stories together in your mind based on what you hear from others. Johnny would be twenty-three, but in my mind he is a six-year-old. To me he has never grown up, he isn't called John, but remains to everyone in my family as Johnny. I always wonder what he would be like. Where would he have gone to school? What would he look like? To this day I picture him as super tall with his white-blonde hair. But I can't be sure.

As a child, I never grieved the loss of Johnny. Around the age of twelve, I entered what was the most difficult time in my life of dealing with Johnny's death. I was angry with God, thinking, "Why would you put my family through so much pain, and how could you be capable of doing that to an innocent child?" I was bitter, because it seemed everyone around me knew him except for me, and he was my brother. Shouldn't I have known him more than anyone? I distinctly remember the feeling of guilt I had. I thought it was selfish of me to cry and grieve the loss of my brother when I wasn't even aware of his death at the time. I hadn't had to experience the pain of losing him the way my siblings did, the way my parents did.

With each passing birthday or anniversary, thoughts of Johnny flood my mind. After sorting through a lot of the confusion that I used to have concerning his death, I sometimes talk to him as if he is very much alive. I have written to him before, and I recently read a journal entry I made to him:

10/19/10. Dear Johnny, Happy Birthday! If I were honoring you from heaven, I would say thank you for laughter, strength, and perseverance, but mostly your guidance. The rainbow is your sign. Whenever I see a rainbow I think of you. Please continue to watch over me. I love you, Johnny, and I wish I knew you. Love, Nicole.

I know he is always with me. To this day, whenever I see a rainbow I think of him and I know he sees me. His memory is still alive in my family. Sometimes I see my mom looking at his picture and I know she is thinking about him. I still pray to him before every test I take in school.

There is a part in my dad's book when he says that Johnny loved holding me and that his kisses are all over my face. I would look in the mirror and see my face and think, "Johnny kissed this face." I would see my eyes and think, "These are the same eyes that saw Johnny alive." I feel blessed that I was alive when Johnny was alive. Even if I didn't know him, at least he knew me.

I have learned so much from Johnny's death, although it's not really a lesson, it's more a way of living that I've taken on. I know how important family is. I know that in any situation I encounter in the future, my family will love me and stand beside me. They are the foundation on which I can stand, and to my parents I am forever grateful. I have learned to trust in God even when I have no clue what is going on. There are so many things in life that I don't understand, but I have faith that everything happens for a reason and that every person on earth has a purpose. Johnny had a purpose that he fulfilled in six short years. I have hope that, one day, I will see him again—hope that one day, the confusion about his death that has clouded my mind will become clear. I love my brother and I miss him every day, but I know that no matter what happens to me, I have an angel in heaven who is always looking out for me.

KATIE

13 years old. She was not yet born when Johnny died.

I'm the fifth daughter in our family. Even though I was not alive when Johnny was, I still feel like I know him as a best friend. I love to think about him and imagine what he would be like today. I picture him as a tall, handsome big brother watching over me all the time with a big smile on his face. I've often thought to myself that I am so unlucky that I never got a chance to know Johnny. I feel like it's not fair that everyone else remembers him and I don't. That everyone else got to touch him and laugh with him and play with him, except me. This is the most difficult thing for me to deal with. But then I remember that God does these things for a reason. He knows what is best for me and I have to trust Him. Don't get me wrong: I still get upset that I don't remember him and that I never got to meet him, but I know when I finally do, it will be one of the greatest days of my life. It's strange to think about how someone I've never met could have such a great impact on me. From everything people have told me about him, I feel as if I have spent a lifetime with him. I laugh with my family at the funny memories of Johnny, and cry with them when we miss him. I always say that I am one of *nine* children; that I have *three* older brothers. I never leave Johnny out.

It's a great comfort to me knowing that I have a big brother in heaven looking after me. Johnny's life has taught me that we never know when our time is coming. He has shown me that I should live my life as if I were to go at any time and meet Jesus face to face. Despite all the pain and sorrow experienced by my family through his death, the joy of knowing that we have our special saint in heaven greatly surpasses that sorrow. It's pretty amazing to be able to say that my brother is in heaven.

Johnny's death has affected me in the way I think and do things, in the way I view people and in the way I pray. He has made an indelible mark on my heart, and I know he would have been an awesome brother. I love Johnny more than words can even begin to explain, and not a day goes by that I don't think about the short, but great, life he lived. Johnny's death has made our family so much stronger. I know that I can always count on any of my brothers and sisters. I am grateful to my parents for putting family life first and for sharing their memories of Johnny with me, because I don't have any of my own. They have made his life a big part of my own. I thank God for putting me in this family: I couldn't even imagine not being a part of it. As our family says: "We're a family—we stick together." This is so true. All eleven of us stick together . . . all the time.

MARIA
12 years old. She was not yet born when Johnny died.

Life without Johnny has been very difficult for me. Often when someone says his name, it brings tears to my eyes. Even though I never met him, I feel as if I have a strong and close relationship with him. People say, "Oh, you look just like him," or, "that sounds exactly like something Johnny would have said." I'm also close to my brother Dave, who was his best friend. I sometimes ask God, "Why did it have to be him? Why couldn't it have been someone else? Why pick us to mourn? What did we ever do to you?" Then I think, "What would life be like with Johnny? Would he have a girlfriend? Would he go to college? Where would he live? We would be a lot happier for sure if he was here." Yes. But he still is—he's just not alive here on earth.

My father's parents and our great-aunt, whom we were particularly close to, have passed away in the last two years, but I know they are in heaven with Johnny, watching over me. If I could make one wish, it would be that Johnny hadn't died and we hadn't had to go through this tragedy. I think, "Why couldn't that driver or God have controlled the car? Why?" That's all I want to know. Why can't God just answer me? Why can't I be angry with God—He took away my brother. I know God did this for reason and that He has a plan. I'm just happy that my brother is saint in heaven. I love and miss him and can't wait, at the end of time, to see him face to face. Even though he's not here physically, he's here spiritually. We are so much alike—we would have had so much fun together, and we *will* have fun in heaven together, he and I together, forever.

~

Gregory is fifteen years older than Maria, and Johnny has been dead for fifteen years. Between the span of ages and the span of time there are bound to be many different experiences of their brother, from the older kids who knew him well to the youngest who were not even alive when he died. Needless to say, I waited with interest to read what they would say. Their reflections move from direct experiences to thoughts, memories and what I would call "imaginings." I am grateful for their words because they reveal their journey to wholeness and holiness, along with the bumps and bruises, the missteps and detours, that accompany such a journey. Johnny's death is still not a neatly wrapped-up reality for

241

them. It still has a quality of unfinished business. This does not worry me, because the passage from this life to the next is *the* great mystery, whatever the circumstances that surround it.

Some experiences are unique to them as individuals; some are more "collective." I hear their anger. I understand their sense that there has been a tear in the fabric of our family. I see their need and their attempts to keep him close. I see their imagination at work, wondering what he would have looked like, who he would have become, how they would have related to him. I am humbled by the bond they have with Maureen and me and the bond they have with each other, knowing at what great cost that bond was forged. I see, in some of them, their need to "make the world right" because their world was shattered. In all of this, Johnny is part of their legacy, and they need to bring that legacy forward with them as they grow up and head out into the world.

I am grateful that they are mainly free of the pain of losing him; that healing has indeed come to them. I am also forcefully struck by many of their comments, particularly those of the four youngest girls, who really didn't know him. I feel their sense of having been robbed ("I have not one personal memory of him") and at the same time, their comfort in knowing he is still part of our family and very much alive, though not here. I see that their relationship with him is mediated through the rest of the family, and realize that there's an oral history going on here that has been going on since the beginning of the world; an oral history by which he becomes alive to them. It is something very Biblical as well: God is known by the stories that are passed from one generation to the next and not only become part of the collective memory of the people but are owned by each generation as their truth, their foundation, their legacy. Think of St. Paul writing to the Corinthians: "For what I received I passed on to you…(1 Corinthians 15:3 NIV); or his exhortation to Timothy: "You then, my son, be strong in the grace that is in Christ Jesus, and what you have heard from many witnesses entrust to faithful men who will be able to teach others also (2 Timothy 2:1-2, RSV, Catholic edition)." Johnny is alive to the younger ones, and indeed to all of us, through story and memory. That is a precious gift, until the day when memory is no longer needed, and yields to the presence of their brother and the Lord that he so loves. As I wrote in the song for my mother's funeral:

O come the day, and come the hour
When we shall be together
And all be one in you our God
Beloved Lord and Master.

TWENTY-ONE

Turn It All to Gold

Fifteen years ago, Johnny entered eternal life. That one glowing ember that said "I will carry you" has carried us ever since. It is an image of the light of Christ, the light that shines in our minds and hearts so that we may experience and share His own radiance with the world around us. That ember, once so pale, like the dimly burning wick of Isaiah (Is. 42:3 RSV), has again become the torch that guides our path. Johnny's death has taught us many lessons about life. And what are those lessons? What "remains," fifteen years out? A few final thoughts, gleaned from a journey that isn't over yet:

Grief. Grief is a long, hard road. But it is a journey, not a destination. You don't end with grief. You end by looking into the eyes of a God who can say, like no one else: I understand. You end by resting in the embrace of One who loves you perfectly, One whose love is bigger than all your pain, all your anger, all your fear. Grief does not have the last word: God does. And in His presence, you find rest for your soul and a place to lay your head, a place to let go of the pain, a place to have your hope renewed. We have a rich life despite our loss, and God uses our loss to make more modest our expectations of what this life can offer, to deepen our desire for heaven, and to impel us to reach out beyond ourselves to ease the suffering of those around us, both near and far.

Suffering. Suffering is related to evil, and evil is a mystery. It is not the only mystery and certainly not the biggest mystery, but it is a mystery nonetheless. A mystery isn't solved like a math problem is solved. A mystery isn't so much solved as it is entered into. It does not admit of precise delineation or rational analysis. It is not finished, wrapped up, and stored away like last year's taxes. Rather, mysteries have a way of opening out before us in ways that widen the horizons of our lives, expanding not only our thinking, but our living. The biggest mystery, the Paschal Mystery, embraces the suffering, death, and resurrection of the Lord as one. In the mind of the Scriptures and the mind of the Church these are not segregated moments. The Paschal Mystery is more like a symphony in which the various movements blend into a harmonious whole.

Why is this important? Because we can never separate the love of God the Father from the love of the Son. Who can say that the Father didn't suffer more than the Son as He watched Him take on the sin of the world and die under its weight? What human mind can comprehend the Father's allowing this to happen to His Son? Yet, what son ever loved a father as the Son of God loved His? We are forever confronted by a love too profound to grasp: the Father, who allowed his Son to take on all the evil of the world, and the Son only too eager to take on that evil out of love for the Father. Not even eternity itself will bring us the full understanding of such love: there will always be more to know, to taste, to experience! God the Father never saw the suffering and death of His beloved Son apart from the Resurrection. And He never sees His resurrected Son without seeing the suffering that He endured for us, the Son whose wounds now shine like jewels.

The answer to the problem of suffering isn't logical deduction. It is a mystery. It is the mystery of the all-good, all-powerful, all-loving Son of God hanging on a cross. We understand the mystery only by standing under the mystery: by standing under the cross. We make sense out of suffering only by contemplating the crucified Son of God, the innocent lamb without blemish, hanging on the cross. Suffering is a great teacher. It can curb our vanity and conceit. It can make us realize what's important and what's not. It can teach us humility. It can wrest from us our illusory sense of "control" of our lives. It can lead us to prayer and surrender. And it can motivate us to reach out to heal the suffering around us.

Healing. The pain diminishes. The horror recedes. With the passage of time there is healing. There is acceptance of what has happened. In the Lord, there is peace: "he is our peace," St. Paul reminds us (Eph. 2:14 RSV). Intense grieving comes to an end. In the early years, Johnny was much more dead than alive: now, in conversation and in memory, he is more alive than dead. That doesn't mean we never grieve his loss. It means that the season of grief, whatever its length, yields to the season of acceptance and growth. The new "norm" for normal remains, and that includes a wound that is never fully closed, never fully scarred over. This is how it's supposed to be. Suffering is a kind of raw gift that keeps us open, both to the unfinished nature of life on earth and to the pain of those around us. We don't expect that wound to fully disappear until we leave this earth. You learn to dance with a hole in your heart.

I now think of Johnny without pain. There will always be moments that sneak up from behind, but they are the punctuation points, not the text of our lives. Joy has returned, the joy that waited patiently for permission to enter and take up residence again in our souls.

Children. Children heal. We realize, with enormous gratitude, that our children are, for the most part, emotionally healthy and well-adjusted. Are they marked by this experience? Of course. They are possessed of certain sober insights about life. We still live with fears and knee-jerk reactions that may never entirely disappear—parking lots, crazy people, evil people, perverts, possibilities for disaster. The bottom line to them all is the question, "what if they die?" And behind the bottom line is the thought, "I could not do this again." And this is a cross we carry all the time, especially when our own children roll their eyes and think we're over-protective, and we keep our mouths shut rather than say something that would terrify them.

Our children are a precious gift, but they are only on loan to us. They were created by God for His purposes, not ours. We can't re-do our lives through our children. We do best by letting them be who God made them to be.

Detachment. I will forever be struck by a comment a friend made years ago: "We're all addicted to looking good." We're trying not to care too much what other people think. We are learning the wisdom of T. S. Eliot's line, "Teach us to care and not to care; and suffer us not to mock ourselves with falsehood." Many things don't matter anymore—at least in our truer moments. But the moments matter and the people who fill those moments matter. We want to seize moments with each other, our children, our friends, Maureen's parents. We have given God permission to heal and change us and given ourselves permission to laugh, to feel, to enjoy, to take time and use it for the important relationships in our lives.

Prayer. One famous writer on prayer said, "Pray as you can, not as you can't." I think we are praying more honestly as a couple. We pray our way through the shadows and disappointments, our sin and our limitations. We have prayed our way through the anger and the desolation, not just the praise. But I think God has enabled us to pray through these emotions and experiences to a new place, a place of deeper realism and deeper hope. My hunch is that we were probably praying most genuinely when we least knew it.

Consolation. God will console you. Ultimately, He is the only one who can. "The LORD is near to the broken-hearted, and saves the crushed in spirit" (Ps. 34:18 RSV). Why can He console you? Because God is a bereaved parent. God is a father who lost a son. If you keep Him away from your grief you cut yourself off from the source of your healing. God doesn't do harm. If you're all-loving you can't do evil. Sin does harm. Evil does harm. We live in a broken, fragile world where terrible things happen to people. We live in between the "already" and the "not yet." Already the world is redeemed by Christ, but the full impact of that redemption will not be felt until the end of the world. Meanwhile, we struggle, and life is a battle. But we struggle in the sure knowledge that the One who is risen from the dead is on our side.

Heaven. Heaven is the only criterion of success. To miss it is to be the most dismal of failures. As a friend of mine in Dublin said, "I don't just want to share my gifts with my children. I don't just want to share my wealth or my intellect or my possessions with my children. I want to share eternal life with my children!"

If the one you love is in heaven, alive, in the total perfection of everything he was created to be, in the fullness of peace, love, joy, and beauty, wouldn't you do *anything* to see him again? If it meant giving up anger, or bitterness—if that were the price to pay—wouldn't you do it in a flash? If it meant re-orientating your entire life to be focused on serving others rather than consumed by your pain, wouldn't you do that? Would you dare risk not seeing him by staying away from the very things that will bring you to him? I discovered I would do anything it took to see my son—anything.

The Body of Christ. We are members of His body. The Church and the sacraments are vehicles of grace. Many years ago, Maureen and I had the same experience within a week of each other. Kneeling before the Lord after receiving Holy Communion, I came to see that Johnny is one with the Lord in heaven, and at Holy Communion I am one with the Lord on earth. In the Eucharist, Christ comes to us: heaven touches earth. In that moment I am one with Christ and Johnny is one with Christ. I kiss my son in the Eucharist. This is comfort. This is consolation. This isn't something dreamed up by my grieving mind. This is reality.

Faith. Faith is a very precious gift, available to all who ask for it. Faith turns death from an ugly, hideous, mocking, gaping hole into a doorway, a doorway through which we move to unending life. One day, death will be over. One day, death will die. One day, there will be no more tears. One day, we will be reunited, if we remain with the Lord. The verse of one of the songs I wrote early on comes back to me again:

And when I settle in for a thousand-year glance
You then point with a motion so fair
You say "I'm not the one that you really desire
Look now, He's right over there."

I see light, like a river of fire
I see love, like a burning desire
I see Christ, with His heart open wide
And his arms outstretched for me.

Ultimately, the beauty of the created souls we love will lead us to the unimaginably beautiful, uncreated beauty of God. And when we see Him, we will finally find our joy, our glory, and our rest.

ABOUT PARACLETE PRESS

WHO WE ARE

Paraclete Press is a publisher of books, recordings, and DVDs on Christian spirituality. Our publishing represents a full expression of Christian belief and practice—from Catholic to Evangelical, from Protestant to Orthodox.

We are the publishing arm of the Community of Jesus, an ecumenical monastic community in the Benedictine tradition. As such, we are uniquely positioned in the marketplace without connection to a large corporation and with informal relationships to many branches and denominations of faith.

WHAT WE ARE DOING

Books Paraclete publishes books that show the richness and depth of what it means to be Christian. Although Benedictine spirituality is at the heart of all that we do, we publish books that reflect the Christian experience across many cultures, time periods, and houses of worship. We publish books that nourish the vibrant life of the church and its people—books about spiritual practice, formation, history, ideas, and customs.

We have several different series, including the best-selling Paraclete Essentials and Paraclete Giants series of classic texts in contemporary English; A Voice from the Monastery—men and women monastics writing about living a spiritual life today; award-winning poetry; best-selling gift books for children on the occasions of baptism and first communion; and the Active Prayer Series that brings creativity and liveliness to any life of prayer.

Recordings From Gregorian chant to contemporary American choral works, our music recordings celebrate sacred choral music through the centuries. Paraclete distributes the recordings of the internationally acclaimed choir Gloriæ Dei Cantores, praised for their "rapt and fathomless spiritual intensity" by *American Record Guide,* and the Gloriæ Dei Cantores Schola, which specializes in the study and performance of Gregorian chant. Paraclete is also the exclusive North American distributor of the recordings of the Monastic Choir of St. Peter's Abbey in Solesmes, France, long considered to be a leading authority on Gregorian chant.

Videos Our videos offer spiritual help, healing, and biblical guidance for life issues: grief and loss, marriage, forgiveness, anger management, facing death, and spiritual formation.

Learn more about us at our website:
www.paracletepress.com, or call us toll-free at 1-800-451-5006.

SCAN TO READ MORE

You may also be interested in . . .

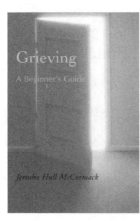

Grieving:
A Beginner's Guide

There is no sure route through grieving. Jerusha McCormack provides instead a series of signposts by which we may find our own path to a new life. "We are all amateurs at grief," she writes, "it comes to us all; we must all go through it. To treat grief as a problem to be fixed, or (worse still) to medicalize it, is to rob us of the extraordinary privilege of encountering this experience on our terms: for each of us has our own way of grieving, and each of us has something special to learn from the process."

ISBN: 978-1-55725-493-1
$14.95, Trade paper

Daily Prayer for Times of Grief

"As heat and pressure make diamonds out of coal, so pain and prayer have made this book a priceless gem."
—Robert Owens Scott, Director, The Trinity Institute

Drawing on her own experience of losing her young husband to cancer, Lisa B. Hamilton offers the practice of fixed-hour prayer for those who mourn.

ISBN: 978-1-61261-128-0
$14.99, Trade paper

Available at bookstores everywhere
Paraclete Press   1-800-451-5006
www.paracletepress.com

You may also be interested in . . .

NEW FROM PARACLETE VIDEO

GUIDANCE FOR WHEN THE UNTHINKABLE OCCURS

Grieving the Sudden Death of a Loved One

Grieving the Sudden Death of a Loved One: Guidance for When the Unthinkable Occurs provides a full hour of support, wisdom, and counsel from experts of many backgrounds including Dr. Earl A. Grollman, the "Hero of The Heartland" for his work with the families and volunteers of the Oklahoma City bombing, and Gregory Floyd, author of *A Grief Unveiled.*

There is no adequate preparation for dealing with the sudden death of a loved one. This video will take you through seventeen segments from *The impact of a sudden death* to *The pain of reality* to *Yielding to the season of grief.* You will hear expert advice about how *Everyone grieves in their own way, How children grieve, Our environment influences how we grieve,* and the ways that *Circumstances can affect grief.* You will learn to *Work through grief,* how *Grief can affect us physically, How to take care of yourself,* and the dangers of *Avoiding grief.* There are what experts call *Grief bursts* and *Holidays and special days* when the feelings will be most intense. Above all, remember that *Grief has no timeframe,* and can last a lifetime. It is okay—in fact, it is healthy—to ask serious questions such as, *Where is God?* And, if you are attempting to care for someone else who is grieving, you need to understand *How to be with someone who is grieving.* Healing will come. Give it time. With this new resource you will discover how to slowly *Move towards acceptance.*

ISBN: 978-1-61261-241-6
$59.95
Length: 60 minutes
Includes insert: Complete by-segment discussion guide

Available wherever DVDs are sold,
call 1-800-451-5006, or visit www.paracletepress.com